getting into

US &
Canadian
Universities

trotman

getting into

US & Canadian Universities

Margaret Kroto

Getting into US & Canadian Universities

This first edition published in 2008 by Trotman Publishing, a division of Crimson Publishing Ltd., Westminster House, Kew Road, Richmond, Surrey TW9 2ND

© Trotman Publishing 2008

Previously published as *Getting into American Universities* by Trotman and Co Ltd in 2004, 2006

Author: Margaret Kroto

British Library Cataloguing in Publication Data
A catalogue record for this book is available from the British Library

ISBN 978 1 84455 168 2

Typeset by Newgen Imaging Systems Pvt Ltd
Printed and bound by The Cromwell Press, Trowbridge, Wiltshire

Contents

About the Author

Margaret Kroto has been a careers practitioner for 35 years, 23 of these as the careers information and publications manager for a careers company. During this time she has produced many local publications and written articles for national directories. She has lived, worked and travelled extensively in North America.

Introduction

This book gives an overview of the education systems and higher education opportunities for UK students in the United States and Canada and is designed to provide information for individuals who are considering this route, and for their advisers and teachers. The main focus is on choosing and getting into undergraduate programmes, but sections on exchange programmes and postgraduate courses are included as these are excellent alternatives for which some form of funding is more likely to be available. Many of the graduate students interviewed felt that it was a great pity that so few British students were aware of the extensive opportunities for postgraduate study and would like to see these more widely publicised.

The United States and Canada are vast countries with some common features and some major differences. In area, Canada is the world's second-largest country (after Russia), but its population has only recently passed 31 million, which is roughly the same as that of the state of California. The United States, on the other hand, is slightly smaller in area than Canada and is the third largest country but has a population of more than 298 million.

Both the United States and Canada welcome applications from international students and there are many of them from all over the world studying in both countries so you will certainly not be alone. Both countries have very large immigrant populations and are, as a result, diverse and multicultural. Many people from the UK have settled in both countries and the fact that they have a common border makes it easier for students to travel widely in both countries. Both have outstanding national parks, lakes, mountains and beaches as well as some great cities.

The recent fall in the value of the US$ against the £ sterling means that your money will go a lot further in the United States, although you must bear in mind that this situation is subject to change. Currency values fluctuate, and in this book figures are quoted in the local currency.

Although the United States tightened its visa application procedure after the tragedy of 9/11, the government has been very anxious to do everything possible to minimise the effects on potential students and to make it as easy as possible to obtain a visa.

None of the students interviewed for this book regretted coming to Canada or the United States. If you are well prepared and well informed you are more likely to make a sound choice.

Good luck!

With thanks to students, and admissions and international service staff at Florida State University, the University of California at Santa Barbara, Harvard University, the University of Connecticut, the University of Pennsylvania, MIT (Massachusetts Institute of Technology) and Dalhousie and Queen's universities in Canada.

Part I
Undergraduate study

01 Why study in the United States or Canada?

There are many attractions to studying in another country, and North America is a popular choice for English-speaking students as there is no language barrier. If you take the time to investigate all the options thoroughly and are aware of all the implications, particularly financial, you will be able to make a realistic and positive decision. You will need to start the process earlier than you would for a course in the UK as it takes time to gather the information, make your choice, or choices, of course and institution, complete the application procedure and then apply for your visa or study permit once you have been accepted. It is recommended that you apply at least a year in advance, but individual institutions will have different requirements.

■ Some advantages

- You will experience a different culture and lifestyle.
- You will have a very broad education and often a wider choice of options.
- In Canada the system varies and can be closer to the US one or to the UK one.
- You will have a very wide choice of institutions and courses.
- You will experience a different system of education.
- Entry to some colleges may be possible with five GCSEs or equivalent.
- Some courses are not available in the UK.
- In the United States it is not difficult to change your choice of major subject in the first two years as you are admitted to the university and not to a specific course. In most Canadian universities you will be admitted to a course.
- Americans and Canadians are generally friendly and welcoming.
- Both countries are multicultural with very diverse communities and campuses.
- The climate may be more appealing in some areas.
- Both countries are vast and offer the opportunity to experience many different environments and activities.

- It could give you an advantage if you wish to live in the United States or Canada and your area of expertise is in demand.
- If you are a top athlete or especially gifted you could get a scholarship.
- Canada is a bilingual country and some universities offer instruction in both English and French.

Possible disadvantages/other considerations

- Undergraduate courses normally take four years in the United States and you may find that you have already covered some of the work done in the first two years. In Canada undergraduate courses are three or four years.
- Regardless of your qualifications you must normally reach a specified level in critical reading, writing and Maths tests (SAT or ACT). Some institutions also require SAT subject tests. This does not apply to UK students applying to Canadian universities.
- You will have regular homework and assignments and be required to attend all classes.
- It is very expensive for international students, even in public institutions.
- You will need a student visa or study permit, which may not be renewed if you are not progressing.
- There is no national health system in the United States and insurance is a mandatory extra. Canada has provincial health-care systems and some do cover international students.
- Some campuses are extremely large and this may not suit everyone.
- Although you may work on campus, there are work restrictions.
- Law, Medicine, Veterinary Medicine and Dentistry are postgraduate courses in the United States and in Canada they require a minimum of two years undergraduate study. In both countries opportunities are limited for overseas students.
- You may not wish to study subjects you left behind after GCSEs or equivalent and this is likely to be required in the United States.
- There are no student bars on campus as the legal age for drinking alcohol is 21.

Some background cultural and educational facts

Both the system of education and the culture in Canada are often said to lie somewhere between the UK and the United States and this can make Canada an appealing choice for British students. This, together with the fact that several international surveys have ranked Canada as one of the best and safest places to live and one of the most multicultural nations in the world, makes it worth looking at the options available. It is a bilingual country, with French spoken as the main language in the province of Quebec and in small communities in other provinces.

On the world stage Canada has a lower profile than the United States as the population is so much smaller and this will certainly appeal to some people whereas others will find certain aspects of the United States more appealing. The quality of higher education in the major universities in both countries is comparable to that of the UK and some of the top universities in the United States rank amongst the best in the world and have reputations second to none. The Canada Foundation for Innovation has recently set up a fund of £12 million to enable Canadian universities to attract the brightest academics from around the world to the top 40 or so universities.

02 The system of education

■ High schools

The education system in the United States is quite different from that in the UK as students are required to study a broad range of subjects in order to graduate from high school. The high-school diploma is not based on a national examination system equivalent to A levels, but awarded to students who successfully complete assignments and pass tests (mostly multiple choice) in a specified range of subjects. Some schools offer Advanced Placement examinations for more able students and some offer the International Baccalaureate (IB).

Students are continually evaluated and graded on their performance in tests, assignments, projects, class discussions, etc. Grades range from A (excellent) to F (fail). Most students graduate with a high-school diploma when they have completed Grade 12. The nearest equivalent in the UK is at least five GCSEs in a broad range of subjects, including Maths (known as 'Math' in the United States), English, a science, a social science/humanities subject and a foreign language.

■ The grading system

Grades are awarded for each credit hour (see Appendix 1) in the American system, both in high schools and in universities, so that it is important for students to attend classes to maintain their Grade Point Average (GPA).

Standard	Grade	Points
Excellent	A	4.00
	A-	3.75
Good	B+	3.25
	B	3.00
	B-	2.75
Average	C+	2.25
	C	2.00
	C-	1.75

(Continued)

(Continued)

Standard	Grade	Points
Poor/minimal pass	D+	1.25
	D	1.00
	D-	0.75
Failure/unsatisfactory	F or U	0.00

In cases of incomplete work, grade points are not awarded. The interpretation of grades can vary slightly.

Occasionally, a scale of 5 is used. The GPA is calculated by dividing the total number of points by the number of credit hours taken. An overall minimum GPA of 2.00 is required to graduate.

Universities

The system mirrors that of high schools, with continuous assessment and the building up of credits. It continues to be based on a broad range of subjects for the first two years of the degree programme, and students then concentrate on their chosen major subject for the final two years. Although you will normally be asked to choose a major subject when you apply, it is usually possible to change fairly easily during the first two years. Some institutions, including the very prestigious Stanford University, welcome outstanding students who are undecided about their major subject, as this is often an indication of all-round ability and an open mind. For international students, however, the US Educational Advisory Service in London recommends that for visa purposes, students should declare a major. Students must take a broad range of subjects, including Maths, English, a science subject, a language (which could be American Sign Language, if available and unless otherwise specified) and a humanities or social science subject. The first two years could, therefore, be considered to be broadly equivalent to an A level course, but in a wider range of subjects. The first year could be considered to be equivalent to a Higher and the second to an Advanced Higher in the Scottish system. The curriculum for the first two years is frequently referred to as 'The Liberal Studies Program' and is designed to give breadth to a student's academic experience. Many universities operate a semester system, with most students completing two semesters a year and using the summer to take paid employment. It is usually possible to take courses in the summer semester if desired. Some universities use a 'quarter' system, dividing study periods into four terms.

The student in the following case study has a sister at Oxford and offers some comparisons between the systems.

I am majoring in Economics and will be graduating soon and working for a private equity firm in London, which I am extremely excited about. Harvard in particular is very good at placing students in finance and consulting positions. Despite the market conditions this year most of my friends are going into banking or consulting. Having gone through recruiting, I am under the impression that firms look favourably upon international students as it separates them from the crowd.

I went to The King's School Canterbury and I would say that most British students here went to a private school. That said, the admissions office at Harvard is actively visiting state schools and trying to encourage less privileged students to apply. I did apply to UK universities and would have gone to LSE if I had not come to Harvard. I chose to come to Harvard for the broad education and a different experience. I was primarily attracted to the name, but the course and opportunity to study in an exciting environment with so many extra-curricular activities in a very diverse student environment made it an offer impossible to turn down.

For the most part I used the Internet to find out about American universities and also called the admissions office at Harvard a few times. I had an interview in London with one of the Harvard alumni living in the UK.

I had no problem with SAT exams I sat or any difficulty in obtaining a visa.

Finding somewhere to live was never an issue as I have lived on campus all four years, just like 99% of the student population at Harvard. It is a different culture, but people were very friendly so it was easy to settle in.

It is difficult to articulate the tangible culture differences. I do think that some people would struggle to adjust, whereas others would thrive. I guess the first thing that struck me was the slang and I sometimes felt as if I was learning a new language. Most universities have fraternities or similar types of clubs, which would not happen in the UK. American colleges also take their sport extremely seriously in comparison to UK universities. I believe Ohio State's annual sports budget is around $110 million.

There are vast differences between higher education institutions in the two countries. My sister is currently at Oxford and we have had completely different experiences. Firstly, I think the course is excellent over here. As the course is a year longer, I have had the opportunity to take all sorts of classes, including History, Arabic Literature and Film Studies, while concurrently majoring in Economics. It is great for those who are undecided on what direction they want to take their studies, as there is so much choice. In terms of my actual living standard everything is taken care of up front and the dining hall food is excellent, serving three meals every day. Some dorms can be a little crammed, while others are luxurious. I feel there is a bit more structure and effort to make student life easier. We have an office of career services, which really simplifies the recruiting process for after college. Social life is very different, mainly just due to the difference in cultures. I have enjoyed a fantastic social life over here, but it has been completely different to my sister's experience. Perhaps the only aspect of university where I would favour the English system is that we constantly have papers and exams that count towards our final degree. That said, I think people end up getting a lot more out of their degree as a result.

I have no regrets at all as it has been a fantastic experience for me. I really have had a great time over here and think that American universities have so much to offer. I became President of the rugby team here and was able to run a club that was nationally ranked in the top ten and had a fantastic education as well. I have thoroughly enjoyed all my classes. Moreover, the alumni ties here are fantastic and there is no other institution in the world with graduate opportunities like Harvard.

If you are thinking about studying in the US I would say – yes, definitely apply. I feel very strongly that more people should apply to American universities.

TIP

- *Apply to several schools as it is a very competitive process, especially in the Ivy League and other highly ranked institutions. Don't leave it at that but follow up with your application. Call the admissions office and find out what particularly it is about each school that excites you.*

Callum King, Senior
Harvard
(www.harvard.edu)

■ Professional courses

In both Canada and the United States Medicine, Dentistry, Law, Veterinary Medicine and a few other vocational or professional courses cannot be started after high school and a specified number of undergraduate credits are always required, although the number and subjects can vary and you need to look at individual university websites for information. These subjects are frequently restricted to citizens or residents of the country in which the course is located but some institutions do offer a few places to exceptional candidates from other countries. There may be a requirement to have taken an undergraduate degree in the same country and to deposit a specified sum of money in a secure account. There are some shortened programmes for international students who have taken similar courses in their own country. Qualifying examinations are almost always required.

Canada

■ The system of education

Education in Canada is a provincial responsibility and there are many variations between provinces. The quality and value of education in Canada is considered to be remarkably uniform across the country, despite the fact that there is no national accreditation body. Universities are granted charters from provincial governments and the major institutions are all in the public sector. In this respect there is a greater similarity with the UK than the United States where many of the major institutions are in the private sector.

The majority of Canadian students follow their undergraduate degree course in the province in which they reside. Students normally progress to higher education at the age of 18 when they have completed Grade 12 in high school, which is said to be similar in level to Year 12 but in a broader range of subjects. There is no national entrance test and each university sets its own admission standards and assesses applicants individually. Students are graded for the work they do in a similar way to those in the United States. In Quebec the system is different as many students attend post-16 colleges called cegeps (college d'enseignement general et professionel – general and vocational education) after five years of secondary schooling and do a pre-university course there.

The grading and assessment system is closer to that in the United States and grades or percentages will seem very high compared with those in the UK. Some provinces use the US-style GPA whilst most simply refer to percentages or use an A–F system. Whilst a mark of 70 per cent will usually be an A in the UK, 90 per cent would equate to an A in Canada. This has nothing to do with the degree of difficulty and is just a different system of assessment, but it can sometimes give British students a false impression of how well they are doing in the early stages!

Most degrees courses are three- or four-year bachelor degrees and are similar in some respects to the UK and in others to the United States. In some provinces you are required to do four years to obtain an Honours degree, whilst in others this can be achieved in three years as in the UK. Students in Canada, like those in the UK, tend to be admitted to a course where they immediately begin to study their major subject as opposed to an undergraduate school where they follow a broad programme for two years as in the United States. There are, however, some 2+2 (two general years followed by two years study of the major) programmes and also some with one general year followed by three years of more intensive study of the major subject. The year is usually divided into two terms or semesters.

You are likely to experience more regular testing than in the UK, but it varies a lot. Some classes have weekly quizzes, others just a mid-term and final exams. Generally more of the mark is weighted towards work during the term and less on the final exam. Typically, UK final exams are worth 60–70 per cent of the final mark, but in Canada it is more like 20–30 per cent. However, this does vary between provinces and universities.

Some students have reported courses to be almost entirely lecture-based whilst in some cases there are more seminars. This depends a lot on the subject and on the size of the institution. Class sizes tend to vary a lot – from five up to about 50 is usual, although some of the first-year undergraduate classes can be in the hundreds. This is especially true of subjects like Biology and Chemistry as so many students hoping to enter medical school later need to take these. This applies in both Canada and the United States.

03 Choosing a university or college

United States

The United States is a very large country, with some states being larger than Britain, and there are consequently many institutions to choose from. A high percentage of Americans do go on to college and there are more than 2,500 institutions listed in *Peterson's Four-Year Colleges*, one of the most widely used reference sources, which also includes Canadian universities. Guides like this provide information such as the courses offered, number of students, cost, entrance requirements, percentage of students with SAT Reasoning scores over 1,200 percentage in the top 10 per cent of their high school and the percentage of applicants accepted. This will help you to narrow down your choices by selecting schools which match your profile and are consequently more likely to be interested in your application. Do not be put off applying, however, if there is an institution you particularly want to attend, as you may be able to convince the admissions staff of your suitability and motivation.

Some universities offer summer sessions for students who would like to get a taste of study at that institution. Sessions are normally offered between May and August, and information on dates and costs can be found on websites or by direct application.

You should be aware that the US government does not monitor the quality of US colleges and universities, but approves accrediting agencies. You must, therefore, make sure that any college you apply to is accredited by a recognised accrediting agency. Those included in the major college guides are recognised, and the US Educational Advisory Service (see Appendix 2) can also advise on this.

How selective is each institution?

The **most selective** colleges accept between 9 and 25 per cent of applicants. **Ivy League colleges** such as Harvard and Princeton, and other prestigious institutions such as Stanford, come into this category, as do some of the more celebrated public institutions such as the

University of California at Berkeley (UC Berkeley) and the University of California at Los Angeles (UCLA). At these universities, between 75 and 98 per cent of freshmen will normally have been in the top 10 per cent of their high-school class and scored more than 1,310 in the SAT, or over 29 in the ACT.

Many large public universities and good private colleges also have many more applications than places and are **very selective**, but should not be a problem for students predicted to get B and C grades at AS and A levels, or A or B grades in Highers and Advanced Highers in Scotland. More than 50 per cent of freshmen will normally have been in the top 10 per cent of their high-school class and scored over 1,230 in the SAT, or over 26 in the ACT. The acceptance rate is 60 per cent of applicants or less.

The **less-selective** colleges should present no problem to students likely to get offers at less-competitive universities in the UK. Over 75 per cent of successful applicants will normally have been in the top half of their high school and scored over 1,010 in the SAT and over 18 in the ACT. The acceptance rate is 85 per cent of applicants or lower.

At the **least selective** colleges 95 per cent of applicants will be accepted and most freshmen will not have been in the top half of their high school – their SAT combined score is likely to be below 1,010, and the ACT below 19.

Non-selective colleges expect a certain standard, but access is otherwise fairly open.

When interpreting the above figures, you should remember that almost all Americans remain in high school until the age of 18, and it might be more meaningful to rate your position at the time of your GCSEs, or Standard grade qualifications in Scotland. If, for example, the bottom 25 per cent of the students in your school leave at the age of 16, it will subsequently become more difficult to be in the top 10 per cent of the year. The SAT score quoted above is the combined critical reading, writing and Maths scores for SAT Reasoning.

You can find these statistics in major guides.

Unless you have specific reasons for choosing a particular location or college, you should consider a wide range of institutions and not just those that are well known internationally, as they tend to be highly selective and your chances of being admitted are slim unless you are an exceptional candidate. There are over 3,000 four-year colleges in the United States and, whilst the elite are inundated with well-qualified applicants, many others are competing for students. Many good colleges accept all students who fulfil the minimum academic requirements.

American universities tend to put a lot of emphasis on the 'student profile', and their websites will often provide an outline of the type of student that they feel will benefit most from the educational experience their particular institution offers. It is important to look at individual websites as they contain a great deal of essential information to help you to make your decision. You can request printed catalogues or directories, but there is often a charge for these, and similar information is on websites. There are priced services offering to make selections based on the criteria you specify, but if you are willing to take the time to do your own research, there is no reason why you should not make a sound choice without this additional expense. You could, however, take advantage of the annual US undergraduate fair, known as College Day, which usually takes place at the American School in London and is organised by the US Educational Advisory Service which also holds undergraduate seminars (see Appendix 2). You should bear in mind that only around 100 American universities attend this event, but these are likely to be interested in recruiting from the UK as well as from American citizens attending the school.

■ Types of university and college

The terms 'university', 'college' and 'institution' are all used for degree-awarding institutions in the United States, and the term used has no bearing on quality or prestige. Some of the most prestigious institutions are liberal arts colleges or institutes. Universities are generally larger and made up of several schools.

Public universities

Public universities are controlled by the state in which they are located and are often very large. Florida State University (FSU), for example, has over 40,000 students, and others have numbers in the region of 50,000. Although the majority of undergraduates will be local due to the preferential fee structure, FSU, for example, has students from all the other states and 100 other countries. These larger campuses do, therefore, have a cosmopolitan atmosphere. Public institutions are prohibited from any religious affiliation by federal and state law. The state or public universities in the Midwest, west and south tend to have gained stronger reputations than most public universities in the north eastern states, This is largely because the first universities were all private and situated in the north east, where they quickly established national reputations which they have retained. It can be more difficult for a good international student to get into a top public institution than a leading private one, as they are likely to be required by the state which funds them to give priority to qualified in-state students.

Private universities

There are many private universities in the United States and they have the same fee structure, regardless of residence or nationality of applicants. They tend to be very expensive, but are also likely to have more open scholarships for which foreign nationals are eligible to apply. The top colleges attract gifted students from all over the world. Perhaps the most famous of these are the Ivy League universities, which tend to be regarded as the American equivalent of Oxford and Cambridge. They are very competitive. The eight Ivy League universities (all on the east coast) are Brown, Columbia, Cornell, Dartmouth, Harvard, Pennsylvania, Princeton and Yale. There are, however, many other prestigious private institutions outside this group. These include Stanford, MIT (Massachusetts Institute of Technology) and a number of liberal arts colleges.

Liberal arts colleges

Liberal arts colleges tend to be much smaller and can be very exclusive. A liberal arts education is a broad education and the term does not mean that students study only the arts and humanities. In fact, it is really a shortened form of 'liberal arts and sciences'; the curriculum is not very different from that of any other higher education institution and you can major in a similar range of subjects. Liberal arts colleges tend to sell themselves on the fact that they are smaller and more personal. You are likely to have a more sheltered life and to be very much part of a small community. These colleges are usually independent and many have excellent academic reputations. They may have religious affiliations. Some of these colleges (e.g. Massachusetts Five-College Consortium and Claremont Colleges in California) have formed partnerships or consortiums to offer students the opportunity to cross register for courses and to pool resources and share facilities such as a library. The aim is here is to combine the benefits of a smaller college with the advantages of a larger institution.

Single-sex liberal arts colleges

There are now very few single-sex liberal arts colleges, and most are for women students. Some of the original group of very prestigious women's colleges, known as the 'Seven Sisters', have now merged with other institutions, including Radcliffe College, which merged with Harvard in 1999. Amongst the most elite of those that remain as women's colleges are Bryn Mawr (near Philadelphia), Mount Holyoke, Smith and Wellesley (all in Massachusetts). The latter offers students the opportunity to join classes at MIT. Barnard College, a women's college in New York City, is affiliated to Columbia University (see Ivy League). Sweet Briar College in Virginia is another well-established women's college. Students at Mount Holyoke are required to live in college for all four undergraduate years and this will not suit everyone.

Perhaps the best-known men's liberal arts college is Wabash College in Indiana which has only 900 students.

Universities with strong religious affiliations

There are many universities with strong religious affiliations in the United States. They are always private and may be small colleges or universities such as the Protestant Pepperdine in Malibu, or larger institutions such as Brigham Young, the Mormon university in Utah. If you wish to look specifically at colleges with religious affiliations, you can search for these on www.a2zcolleges.com – it covers mainly Catholic, Protestant and Mormon institutions, and you can search by clicking on 'Religion', and then search the whole of the United States or a particular state.

Historically Black Campus Universities (HBCU), Predominantly Black Institutions (PBI) and Traditionally White Institutions (TWI)

You will sometimes see institutions referred to as historically, traditionally or predominantly black or traditionally white, but of course all are now open to everyone who qualifies to study there. The National Association for Equal Opportunity in Higher Education (NAFEO) represents 118 historically black institutions, champions their development and interests and publishes a list of them. Some students do make a positive choice of a historically black institution.

Research universities

A few very prestigious institutions, such as California Institute of Technology (Caltech), are primarily geared towards postgraduate study in the sciences, but do take undergraduates. This is not an official category of university, but top students aiming at research careers may wish to know which universities have a very high percentage of postgraduate students, and which offer no postgraduate study or opportunities for undergraduate research projects. Universities with fewer undergraduates than postgraduates include Caltech, Stanford, Harvard and MIT. Large, highly competitive public universities, such as Berkeley and UCLA in California, also have a larger number of postgraduates than undergraduates. The vast majority of universities and colleges also offer research-based postgraduate courses, but have a higher number of undergraduate students. Some of these are very highly regarded in the research field, and you can generally recognise them by the large number of postgraduates they have (information on this can be found in reference books and on individual websites). You should, however, bear in mind that some undergraduate colleges have carried out some very successful research projects.

Specialist colleges

Whilst the majority of colleges offer a very wide range of courses, some either specialise in, or have developed a particular reputation for, a certain type of course or learning style. Examples are:

■ Art and design – California Institute of the Arts, Cooper Union, Parsons School of Design (both in New York City), School of the Art Institute of Chicago, School of the Museum of Fine Arts (Boston) – in addition many major universities have strong reputations in this area.

■ Music – Juilliard School (New York City), New England Conservatory of Music, Boston Conservatory, Manhattan School of Music, San Francisco Conservatory of Music, Oberlin Conservatory of Music (Ohio) plus many major universities and liberal arts colleges.

■ Drama and dance – New York University, Sarah Lawrence (New York City), Princeton and UCLA (Los Angeles) are not specialist institutions, but are amongst those with outstanding reputations.

■ Film and television – many of those with outstanding schools are in the public sector and include Arizona State, Boston, Michigan State, NYU (New York City), FSU (Tallahassee) and UCLA (Los Angeles). USC (University of Southern California – a very competitive private school in Los Angeles) also has an outstanding film school.

■ Technical institutes – Caltech, Colorado School of Mines, Florida Institute of Technology, Georgia Institute of Technology, Harvey Mudd College (California), MIT, Illinois Institute of Technology and many others.

■ Non-conformist colleges – amongst the best known are Antioch (Ohio), Hampshire, Reed College (Portland, Oregon) and Sarah Lawrence (New York City).

Various guides provide information on specialist colleges, but no list is fully comprehensive, and the information is often subjective. If you do your research thoroughly, you may well find other colleges equally suitable for you. Websites are an excellent source of information. The website www.a2zcolleges.com allows you to search for drama schools, arts colleges and music schools.

American college conferences (not a type of college, but a very important aspect)

Many regional groups of universities belong to special athletics 'conferences' for the purposes of competition and cooperation. Inter-collegiate athletics is a very big thing in American universities and the most competitive are those most likely to offer scholarships to talented athletes. These conferences come under the wing of the NCAA (National

Collegiate Athletics Association) and the NAIA (National Association of Intercollegiate Athletics). The Ivy League (see above) is one of these conferences. Other major conferences are The Atlantic Coast, The Big East, The Big Ten, The Pacific 10 and The Southeastern Conference, which are amongst those in Division 1 of the Football Bowl. American football is the biggest and most lucrative of all sports in US colleges. There are also conferences for many other sports. They may be formed exclusively of private institutions, or a mixture of private and public and compete within the conference to which they belong in the same way as football leagues in the UK. Athletic competition is governed by strict NCAA rules and students need permission to compete elsewhere and will have to adhere to certain rules if they transfer to another university.

Community colleges

Community colleges are non-competitive and offer a variety of two-year courses. Successful students can transfer to a four-year programme at a university and obtain credits for study already completed. Universities in the state system are usually required to accept successful students who are residents of that state. In some cases, American citizens can be regarded as residents of a state when they have lived there for one year, but this does not apply to nationals of other countries. Community colleges are an option for those students who do not have the minimum required qualifications and also tend to be cheaper.

■ Types of undergraduate courses

Bachelor's degree

Most foreign nationals looking for a full-time undergraduate course in the United States will be thinking in terms of a Bachelor's degree (also referred to as a Baccalaureate degree). As has already been stated, this provides a broad education for the first two years, and the study of a major subject for the final two years. Graduates are normally awarded a BA (arts and humanities subjects) or a BS (engineering and science subjects). A BFA (Bachelor of Fine Arts) may be awarded at some institutions for a few subjects, including performance arts. Degrees of distinction may be awarded as follows:

■ Cum Laude – overall GPA of 3.50
■ Magna Cum Laude – overall GPA of 3.70
■ Summa Cum Laude – overall GPA of 3.90.

In the UK system, the majority of students follow an Honours degree programme (e.g. BA (Hons)), but the 'Honors Program' in American universities is normally one that academically talented students elect to follow if they are eligible. At some institutions you would be invited to apply as a freshman, and at others you could choose this option in your junior year if your GPA is above a specified level. Institutions may offer 'general' and 'specialized' Honours programmes – it varies and you would need to enquire. To graduate with honours, you must achieve a specified overall GPA, and write and defend a thesis covering independent work you have done alongside your chosen courses.

Associate's degree

Associate's degrees are two-year courses which are either vocational or the first two years of a Bachelor's programme (broad-based liberal arts). Many of these courses are done in community colleges, and students on the latter option can apply for a transfer to the third (junior) year of a university.

Transfer students

Students who have completed part of a higher education course outside the United States can also apply to an American university as a transfer student. This is dealt with at the end of this chapter, and further details can be found on websites and by direct application.

Professional courses

Courses leading to a specific career are known as professional courses.

■ Location of institutions

If at all possible, you should visit any university you are considering applying to, although most institutions do not require this. Unless you have already travelled widely in the United States, it is risky to undertake such a venture without first-hand information and some knowledge of the area. The United States is, in many respects, a group of countries sharing the same language, but with cultural, environmental and other important differences between them. A small country town in the United States, for example, could be hundreds of miles from another town and difficult to access without transport. You could live in New York or San Francisco without your own transport, but American society relies very heavily on the car, and in many places your lifestyle will be very restricted without one. You will find that some parts of the country may be less tolerant of diversity.

Climate is another issue, as winters can be extremely cold in some places and summer conditions can be extremely hot and humid for several months in other areas. If you find extreme conditions intolerable or suffer from allergies, you will need to take these factors into account. Consider therefore:

- The location of the university – is it in a large town, close to a large town or in a remote situation?
- The climate – is it temperate, or is winter very harsh or summer excessively humid?
- The cultural aspects of the area – what activities are available; is there easy access to theatres, concerts, a wide range of shops, museums, etc.?
- What recreational activities are possible in the area – sailing, skiing, mountaineering?
- What are the living costs in this area? These can vary widely, with major cities and areas where the cost of real estate is high generally being more expensive.
- Is campus accommodation available? This can vary from 100 per cent in some private liberal arts colleges and universities to quite a low percentage in some urban areas.

■ Size of institutions

- What size is the university? This can vary enormously, and larger institutions are likely to have larger classes and may be overwhelming to some people. On the other hand, they may also offer a wider range of courses and activities.
- The largest universities may have more than one campus and are very often in large towns. Some will be in smaller towns where the university dominates the town.
- Smaller colleges may form a more close-knit community, particularly if they are situated in a remote area or very small town.

The student in the following case study looked thoroughly at all options before making his choice.

I grew up in London and attended a private preparatory school until I moved with my father to Brussels at the age of nine. I spent two years in the British School of Brussels before returning to England as a boarder at Dulwich College, an independent school in South London where I completed my GCSEs and A levels, gaining A grades. I have always been a keen sportsman and played 1st XV Rugby for Dulwich. One of the achievements I am most proud of was being elected School Captain – this was a great honour and a fantastic experience to lead and coordinate the student government and interact with the senior staff on almost all matters pertaining to school life.

I first considered applying to study in the US at the beginning of my penultimate year in high school. What attracted me initially was a sense of 'bigger and better' – it was very clear from my initial research that the top Ivy League institutions offer a more involved and personal education than their British counterparts through the vast resources they have available. This was supported by the considerable level of personal interaction I had with US university representatives during the application process in contrast with the fairly impersonal British UCAS system. I was in regular contact with US university reps who made me feel very comfortable with the process and helped to show how US universities could adapt to meet my needs. Besides first impressions, I was particularly attracted to the liberal arts program offered by US universities. During the latter years of high school I kept my academic pursuits relatively broad and was quite concerned by the prospect of having to identify a single subject to study at a British university. The four-year liberal arts program offered in the US thus appealed to me as a way to continue to study a range of subjects and give myself more time to identify which particular subject I would like to focus on. In addition to this, one of the more important factors that encouraged me to apply to the US was a desire to experience something quite different. I believe that university is just as much a social experience as it is an academic training. Moving to the States for university provided a way for me to step off the traditional track slightly and allow myself a more challenging but potentially more rewarding social and cultural experience. I ended up applying to four US universities (Harvard, Yale, Stanford and Princeton) and six UK universities (Oxford, UCL, LSE, Bristol, Durham and Nottingham).

I tried to get in contact with current students at each university to get the inside scoop on what they were like and whether they would suit me. I contacted former students from my school who were attending the universities and the universities put me in touch with people with a similar background. In addition to this informal advice, I considered university league tables as well as advice from contacts I had met through internships or friends.

My choice was ultimately fairly easy. While I was choosing between very comparable universities with regard to their academic reputation, Harvard stood out as somewhere with the highest international reputation. Those who studied there at the time assured me that while it is competitive and challenging, students have a lot of fun and being near a big city, there is a lot to do off the campus.

I did not have a chance to visit the university before coming, but I did have an interview with a Harvard alum during the application process. This is considered a fairly informal part of the application process by the university but it was a good opportunity to ask questions about what Harvard had to offer.

I applied for financial aid and currently receive approximately $38,000 per year to help pay for tuition. In addition my family contributes around $20,000 and I have about $15,000 personal earnings.

Arranging to take the SAT was fairly easy as you can do this through the College Board website. You need to register a month or more in advance. There are a few locations where you can take the SAT in London although the one in central London (the closest to me) books up quickly so you must register quite far in advance. The only difficulty I faced was that SAT tests are only held on Saturdays, which was a little problematic at times as I had school sports matches. Once accepted, the visa process was also relatively straightforward. It simply required that you visit the US embassy in London and present your university admissions documents along with your passport. The whole process took less than a few hours (despite heavy security!) although they kept my passport for a week after my visa interview for processing which forced me to change travel plans I had made.

The biggest difference between the two countries is the US liberal arts program compared to the single-subject degree programme in the UK. The advantage of the US system is that it allows you to continue to study other subjects around your degree all the way through university. One disadvantage might be that you are compelled to take a variety of subjects, some of which you may not be interested in and might not have studied for several years. While I was happy to have the opportunity to study a broad range of subjects, some students do not appreciate being forced to take subjects in which they have little to no interest.

From my experience, the US higher education system is more of an extension of high school than can be said of the British system. This is partly due to the fact that you are studying multiple subjects simultaneously as you do in high school, but there is also more guidance and oversight than at a British university. There is a greater emphasis on taking part in extra-curricular activities such as sports, student government or involvement in any one of the many student societies on campus. I personally think this can only be a good thing as it encourages you to get involved in more activities than you might at a British university. However, this can lead to students (especially in a highly competitive environment such as Harvard) overextending themselves which can get a little overwhelming at busy times of the year.

The biggest difficulty I faced coming the US for university was the cultural difference when it came to social activities and perceptions. It is perhaps regrettable that much of the socialising that takes place in British universities is over a beer in a pub, bar or club. This is clearly not immediately possible in the US due to a higher drinking age and consequently US students have developed other ways in which to socialise and meet new people. This is not necessarily a bad thing, but it has a strangely large impact on European students who are culturally accustomed to having a glass of wine with a meal or a beer on the weekend. It is almost as though European students are taking a social step backwards, with this new restriction making students feel younger than they would at home where most would consider themselves adults. This feeling is compounded by greater restrictions and oversight from the university that certainly make you feel less independent than you might at a British university.

At Harvard I have continued to play Rugby. While it is not quite a mainstream sport, there is a well-established club team that competes throughout the nation. My main extra-curricular activity is with Harvard Student Agencies (HSA), a student-run corporation on campus. HSA is the largest student-run corporation in the world and aims to provide valuable business and management experience to Harvard undergraduates as well as helping them pay their way through college. I have recently been elected President of the organisation and take operational control for one fiscal year. My concentration at Harvard is Economics and I currently have a 3.5 GPA. This form of constant assessment means that your freshman year carries as much weight as your senior year. The system is forgiving in the sense that a bad grade in one semester will not significantly affect your GPA, however, it also means that you are held accountable for every class you have enrolled in throughout your university career. As a UK student accustomed to final exams held once a year, this system takes some time to get used to. However, I now feel that the system has encouraged me to study in a more consistent and sustainable fashion than I had perhaps done previously and has allowed me to cover more material in a single semester.

TIPS

- Before you look at different US universities, it is important to establish in your mind what it is you are looking for from the experience. I would recommend listing your priorities (e.g. academic reputation, sports, social life, extra-curricular activities, campus vs. city, etc.) so that you have valid criteria by which to compare universities.
- It is really useful to speak to current students of the universities you are considering. They are able to give you insight into life at the university that you will not get from any literature or official representative.
- Make sure that you understand the US higher education system and what it entails as it is quite different from that

in the UK. While many find it particularly rewarding and challenging, it is not right for everyone and it can be quite a shock for the unprepared student from the UK.

Timothy (Tim) Creamer, Junior majoring
in Economics
Harvard
(www.harvard.edu)

■ Number of international students at institutions

Whilst the main criteria for choosing a college will be the course and the type of institution, some students may feel more comfortable where there is either a good mix of international students or a number of other students from their own country. It is not always easy to access reliable information on a nationwide basis, but you can request this from each institution you are considering. You could also ask the Educational Advisory Service (EAS) at the Fulbright Commission (see Appendix 2), although they do not make such information available for publication. There are websites which rank universities according to the number of international students, but this will not tell you how many of them are from the UK. India and China have the highest number of students in the United States, followed by Korea, Taiwan and Canada. The United States remains popular with UK students.

The most popular destinations in the United States for international students are California, Massachusetts, New York, Pennsylvania, Ohio, Illinois, Michigan, Minnesota, New Jersey, Florida and Texas.

Information on universities with the highest number of international students can be found in some publications and at:

■ www.edupass.org – access via 'Admissions' and then 'Schoolsearch'.
■ www.iie.org – access via 'Opendoors' on the home page.
■ www.auap.com – produces annual rankings of universities by number of international students. You need to register to access this information.

Edupass lists the top 50 schools with the most international students in alphabetical order, and highlights those which give financial aid. This can still be misleading, as some of those listed take very few international students at undergraduate level, but many postgraduates. The website also gives the top 50 schools with the highest percentage of international students, which brings in many smaller colleges, usually private, with much lower student numbers overall. Many of these are highly selective and include Harvard, MIT, Stanford, Cornell, Dartmouth, Pennsylvania, Bryn Mawr, Madison (Wisconsin), Macalester (Minnesota), Middlebury (Vermont) and Smith (Massachusetts).

The Institute of International Education's website provides various listings, some of which are only available to subscribers. Those listed are in order of the highest number of international students, and include the top 50 for all levels of study, the top 40 for undergraduates and the top 40 for research programmes. You will notice that the undergraduate list (Baccalaureate) is very different when compared with the other two. The same, often prestigious institutions tend to appear on the total number of students and research lists, which makes it apparent that the majority of international students in these universities are postgraduates. Currently 156 institutions have more than 1,000 international students.

Canada

■ Getting started

The best starting point, if you are looking to take a course at one of Canada's major universities, is the official website of the Association of Universities and Colleges of Canada (AUCC) – www.aucc.ca. The AUCC currently has 92 member institutions, all of which are in the public or non-profit sector and all with established reputations. The site has a map of Canada showing the locations of the institutions and lists them by province. You can then access an overview of each, which includes the location, number of students, cost for international students, accommodation and sports offered. Information is given in English or French, depending on the language of instruction at that institution. Once you have identified the institutions which interest you, the next step is to look at their websites for further information.

If you are looking for a non-degree or vocational course then the best initial source is the website of the Association of Canadian Community Colleges – www.accc.ca – which also contains a database. See below for further details.

Remember that the quality of websites varies so it is important to use ones with official accreditation and ignore those which are mainly concerned with advertising a few private colleges, online courses or English language courses. This is true for the United States and Canada.

There is no official league table of universities but there are unofficial rankings, although you need to use these with caution as they attempt to grade an institution as a whole and you are looking at a particular department. The majority of universities in Canada are public as they are in the UK and for this reason there is less variation in quality than is the case in the United States. It is also important to note that the grading is often for the quality of research and, whilst this is important for many subjects as it reflects the quality of the faculty, there may well be teaching excellence and courses of greater interest to you at one or more of those lower in the pecking order. Large universities such as McGill in Montreal, Toronto, University of British Columbia in Vancouver, McMaster in Hamilton and the University of Alberta in Edmonton are almost always featured in the top half dozen. All are very large institutions in urban areas and you may prefer a good university in a smaller place. Queen's University in Kingston, Ontario and Dalhousie in Halifax are examples. Membership of the AUCC is an indication of quality, but this does not necessarily mean that others are of poor quality.

■ Types of university and college

Public universities

All the major universities in Canada are in the public sector and in this respect differ from the United States and equate more closely to the UK system. They are the responsibility of the province in which they are located. British Columbia has 7 universities, Alberta 4, Saskatchewan 3, Manitoba 3, Ontario 23, Quebec 16 (11 of which are branches of the University of Quebec), New Brunswick 4, Prince Edward Island 1, Nova Scotia 8 and Newfoundland 1.

Liberal arts colleges

These tend to be smaller than universities and may be called university colleges. Some are in big cities and some in smaller towns and offer degrees in both arts and sciences like those in the United States. They can be in the public or private sector.

Private institutions

Canada has far fewer private institutions than the United States and most have a religious foundation. Only nine of them offer degree courses. Quest University in Squamish, north of Vancouver, is the newest private non-denominational and non-profit liberal arts and sciences university in Canada and has quickly established a good reputation. It is not yet on the AUCC website as it only opened in 2007 and it takes time to gain the recognition required for membership. It has been approved by the British Columbia Degree Quality Assessment Board as a degree-awarding institution.

There are also private vocational colleges.

Universities and colleges with religious affiliations

These vary in quality and in the courses they offer from province to province. Some are affiliated to public universities and offer a wide range of courses and others are primarily Bible colleges and seminaries, which may still be affiliated to local universities.

Specialised colleges

These are usually in areas such as art and design, engineering, agriculture and theology. The Ontario College of Art and Design in Toronto is the largest in Canada. These colleges may offer certificates, diplomas and associate degrees as well as bachelor degrees.

Community colleges

Community colleges offer technical or vocational qualifications and courses to enable access to university. In general they are more highly developed in the western provinces.

The term 'community college' is a generic one and community colleges may have different names but the key function is to respond to the needs of industry, business and the public service sector and to the needs of students who want a vocational course. They primarily offer certificate and diploma courses and students can transfer to relevant university degree courses after successfully completing a diploma. Some offer associate degrees, which are accepted as the first two years of an undergraduate course for some programmes. A growing number also offer degree courses.

Cegeps are sometimes referred to as the Quebec equivalent of community colleges as they offer a range of general and vocational courses. There are 48 of them in the province and they offer the main route into higher education for Quebec students as regular secondary education is completed after five years. In this respect they differ from the community colleges in the other provinces and equate more closely to a post-16 college in the UK where vocational course students study on the same campus as A level students.

Language of instruction

The majority of universities in Canada offer courses only in the English language except in Quebec where most teach in French, as does one in Manitoba and one in Nova Scotia. Some universities in other provinces have affiliate colleges which teach in French. In Quebec McGill and Concordia in Montreal and Bishop's in Sherbrooke teach in English and the University of Ottawa, a private non-profit university with a Christian background, offers courses in both languages.

■ Location of institutions

The main criteria are the same as listed for the United States.

- Large areas of Canada are virtually uninhabited with the bulk of the population concentrated in the larger cities in the provinces of Ontario, Quebec, Alberta and British Columbia.
- The Maritime Provinces, particularly Nova Scotia, are smaller in area making their population densities larger. Halifax, although relatively small, is the largest city and in many ways the most accessible for UK students as it is closer in both distance and time zone.
- Although the larger universities are located in major cities there are many universities in smaller towns too.
- The climate varies across the country but in most of the major cities it is very cold in the long winters and hot in the shorter summers so temperatures can be quite extreme. In the coastal cities of Vancouver and Halifax the winters are more temperate but they still get snow and winter sports are a major recreational activity across the country.

United States and Canada

◼ Fraternities and sororities

Whilst many aspects of American student life may be similar to that in the UK, fraternities and sororities, together with the 'football culture' at many institutions, may be baffling to British students. Fraternities (for men) and sororities (for women) have a long tradition on the American campus, and are also referred to as 'Greek organisations' as they all have Greek names. They are national organisations and only some of them will be represented at any given university – local groups are known as chapters. You are a member of your particular fraternity or sorority for life, but the majority of people do not remain active after graduation. Students have to apply to join and there is a selection process, which finishes with a secret initiation ceremony for those accepted. There is a charge to belong, and members may live in a house owned by their chapter, or live elsewhere but have all their meals in the house. In many ways they are now social clubs which reflect the interests or backgrounds of members. Although they will usually have philanthropic aims and encourage their members to study hard (with the withdrawal of privileges if their GPA drops below a specified level) and contribute to society, there is a certain amount of scepticism, and non-supporters of the system sometimes describe them as 'partying' organisations.

Greek Life also thrives on the Canadian campus and operates in a similar way to the United States, with dues paid at university and membership for life. Many people use it as a way to make friends and do not stay active after graduating. The emphasis is on community service but also on having fun – www.canadiangreeks.com.

It is worth finding out how strong this tradition is in any universities you are considering, as they can dominate campus life. Some colleges employ directors of Greek Life who are strongly involved with student activities, and many have an office of fraternity and sorority affairs. Typically, a large public university will attract a membership of around 5 per cent of the student body, but it could be 50 per cent in a smaller private college. If Greek Life does not appeal to you, it is worth taking this fact into consideration, as social activities could be more limited for the 'outsiders' where membership is high. Some students become heavily committed to the philanthropic activities of their chapter, some just see them as a way of making friends and having a good social life, and others find them divisive and feel they have no part on the modern campus. Members heavily involved on the organisational side feel that it helps to develop skills which will be invaluable in their future careers. You will have to decide for yourself.

The voluntary fraternities and sororities should not be confused with Phi Beta Kappa and Gamma Phi Beta, as these are 'honor societies' which only the highest achievers are invited to join. Phi Beta Kappa was actually the first fraternity and was founded in 1776.

The freshman in the following case study is thinking about joining a fraternity.

I've always liked America and visited fairly often as my father knew the country through work commitments here and brought us here on occasions. I also attended a tennis camp in Florida so I was fairly familiar with the culture. Quite a few of the major American universities visit my old school (St Paul's in London) every year so it's not unusual for students to apply to them. My cousin and several other former St Paul's students ar e also here and about 10% of A level leavers go to American universities every year. Before making my decision I was lucky enough to have the opportunity to visit eleven major universities and chose Penn as I wanted to be in a campus community in an urban setting. Penn is just across the river from the centre of Philadelphia and the campus has many amenities. I also liked the multi-ethnic aspect and was, of course, attracted by the fact that it is an Ivy League university and that improves your employment prospects a lot.

I made an early decision to go to Penn and was committed as soon as they accepted me. I took the SAT tests at the American School in London and did practice papers first, which I would recommend everyone to do. My school had to provide two references and send a transcript of my A levels which were in French, Maths and Latin. I also had to write an essay and I had an interview with a Penn alum at Starbucks in London, where there is quite a network of Penn alumni. I don't receive any financial assistance so my father had to provide evidence that I would be fully supported before I could get my student visa.

The great thing about the system here is that you can choose different courses every semester for the first two years and don't have to decide on your major area of study before you start your course as you do in the UK. I was admitted to the College of Arts and Sciences and have a fairly wide range of courses to choose from as long as I satisfy the general requirements and take a minimum of 16 courses in my first two years. This semester I chose to take Advanced Latin, Planning to be Off-Shore, Italian Food and Culture and a writing seminar. Initially I chose Chinese but found this very time-consuming as the Latin was taking a lot of my time so I switched to the Italian food course. The planning course fulfils the societal requirement and covers topics such as out-sourcing of labour and economic development. As my Latin course is an advanced one I am studying that alongside some graduate students as well as other students who have a passion for the subject. The requirements can be found on the website and I have to ensure I meet them. There are faculty advisers to help with this.

I have found the standard higher than I expected and have a lot of essays to write as well as mid-term and end of semester examinations. The grading system is very different and you need to get at least 90% to get an A.

You are allowed to work for a limited number of hours on the campus and I have a fund-raising job with the Hillel Jewish Center and work for three hours on two or three days a week. I earn $8.50 an hour and this helps with spending money.

Although I haven't yet joined a fraternity I am interested in doing so when I find one that fits me as I think it's socially advantageous. You have to go through the 'rushing' process where fraternities bid for you as the existing members have to approve your admittance – it's a two-way process and helps you to meet people with whom you have a lot in common. Between 30 and 40% of the students here pledge for fraternities, sororities and secret societies.

TIPS

- *My advice to students thinking about studying in the USA is to be open-minded, to weigh up the pros and cons and to consider what you will get out of it. You must be willing to leave the security of your family and friends, but once you get over that it really is worth it. I miss those people and Arsenal but that is a small price to pay in the pursuit of optimal personal development.*
- *Make sure you keep up-to-date with all your work to avoid letting your GPA drop. If it drops below a specified level you could be put on 'Academic Probation' and could even have your I-20 withdrawn if you are not making satisfactory progress.*
- *Make sure you ask to have your qualifications evaluated to see whether you can apply for any credits.*

James Zimmerman, Freshman
University of Pennsylvania, Philadelphia
(www.upenn.edu)

■ Admission criteria — United States

American students

Universities accept American students on the basis of their GPA for the last three years of high school, the application form and personal statement or essay, references from teachers and counsellors and their SAT or ACT score. The GPA is recorded on an official high-school transcript which is sent directly to all universities a student applies to.

Universities will all have their own criteria for admission, as they do in the UK. The most competitive colleges may expect a high-school GPA of 4.00 and a high score in the SAT or ACT. Typically, a good public university (governed by the state in which it is located) will require a GPA of 3.25 or better on all academic subjects, together with a specified SAT or ACT score. This may sound high, but the American system does not work in the same way as in the UK, and an able student who works hard, completes all assignments and does well in the tests (mainly multiple choice) is likely to be awarded A grades on a fairly regular basis.

Students in some American high schools now take Advanced Placement (AP) tests, which are nationally recognised and awarded by the College Entrance Examination Board (CEEB). There is a system of awarding credits for particular scores in these tests. Where these are offered, students will normally choose one or more subjects to study at an advanced (college) level during the last two years of high school and take tests. There is also a qualification known as the Advanced International Certificate of Education (AICE), awarding AS and A levels, and this must not be confused with the British system. Some university guides include tables showing credits awarded for specified grades at these levels, but it applies only to the AICE which some American high schools offer.

British students

British students are accepted on the basis of their GCSE or Standard grade (Scotland) results, AS/Scottish Higher results and predicted A level grades, test scores (usually SAT), application form and school/college references. Many competitive colleges apply a weighting to courses and may only take into account the subjects they regard as academic. This could be a problem in the case of vocational courses since they do not readily translate to the American curriculum. A case would have to be made on the basis of the academic content of the course, and a detailed analysis of this would have to be submitted.

As the only validated qualifications at the time of application may be GCSE or equivalent examinations, you will generally be expected to have gained at least a grade B in five or more of these for admission to one of the more competitive universities. Subjects should include Maths, English, a science, a foreign language and a social science/humanities subject. The most competitive universities will have much higher requirements, and may also expect a prediction of three grade A passes at A level or equivalent. Some specify a minimum of grade C at A level whilst less competitive colleges may accept lower grades or admit students with GCSE or equivalent only. You will normally be expected to have been in full-time education until the age of 18.

Most British students will have AS and A levels or Scottish Higher/Advanced Higher Grades, and can apply for credits if they achieve good grades. The syllabus sometimes has to be submitted so that the content can be evaluated, and there may be a charge for this. Strong A level results can often be substituted for the AP tests mentioned above, but you usually need to request this. At Yale University, for example, freshmen may be awarded the same credits for A and B grades at A level as they would for top AP test scores. At some institutions, it might even be possible for students with outstanding results (AAA/AAB) to go straight in as a second-semester freshman (or even a sophomore), although they may be required to take some freshman courses in subjects they left behind at the age of 16. Some students who are eligible to apply for exemptions, however, choose to take the full number of credits, either as a refresher course to help them to settle in and become used to the system, or to take some different courses. There are, of course, cost implications as you pay on the basis of the number of courses taken, except in some private institutions where the full fee covers as many subjects as you wish to, and can realistically take.

Whilst many of the larger institutions are familiar with AS and A level examinations, many will not have much, if any, idea about vocational A levels or Scottish Highers/Advanced Highers. Since the Scottish system requires students to take four or five subjects, it equates more closely to the American system of keeping a broad range of subjects open, and is likely to be acceptable when fully explained.

Similarly, if you have more specialist qualifications considered to be equivalent to AS and A levels in the UK (e.g. a BTEC National Diploma), North American universities will not be familiar with these, and you will probably have to apply to have the content evaluated by a recognised independent body if you wish to be considered for admission or claim any credits. There is normally a charge for this.

The International Baccalaureate is a highly regarded qualification that is also offered in some American schools, and most universities will use an established system of evaluation to admit students and to award credits for this.

■ Admission criteria — Canada

Canadian students

At one leading Canadian university 8.3 per cent of students in a popular department entered with a high school graduation mark of 95 per cent and a further 43.1 per cent had an average between 90 and 94 per cent. Typical average marks are between 70 and 80 per cent depending on the course. Some universities will only accept students with an average of 70 per cent or above, but this will vary between institutions and between provinces.

British students

The major universities are the most selective, but all welcome applications from international students and British qualifications are highly regarded. The websites of major universities all have international admissions sections and specify the requirements for students who have had a British-based or British-patterned education. Major Canadian universities will expect a range (at least five subjects) of GCSE/Standard grades at A or B and A/AS/Highers/Advanced Highers at C or above. Sometimes two subjects will be sufficient but some programmes will ask for three in specified subjects and B grades or better may be required. Students may also be admitted with AS levels or equivalent and will require four or six subjects depending on the selectivity of the university. A or B grades at A level or equivalent will be required if you apply for any credits. For example, at the University of British Columbia in Vancouver, where undergraduate courses take four years, you can apply for first-year course credit if you have A or B grades in three A levels or equivalent. The system there is very flexible as students can either commit to a major (or dual major) at the beginning or explore interests for two years as is the norm in the United States.

The International Baccalaureate with a specified grade total in the region of 28 is also very well recognised. Credits may be granted for high grades in appropriate subjects. Websites will usually specify grades required.

■ Students with disabilities

The United States has generally been ahead of many other countries in introducing facilities for disabled students, and you will not be disadvantaged if you have a disability. You should make early enquiries about any special arrangements.

All the major universities in Canada offer services and resource centres for students with disabilities and details of these can be found on their websites. McGill University has compiled a list of 'Access services at Canadian universities' which links to these pages but acknowledges that it is not exhaustive. This can be found at www.mcgill.ca/osd/links.

■ Can I transfer from a degree course in the UK?

International students are generally eligible to apply for admission to a university as transfers if they have graduated from a secondary school and completed one or more semesters of full-time study at a university or other higher education institution, but some universities (e.g. Berkeley) only accept transfer students into the junior year, which requires two years of prior higher education study. Credits are not likely to be awarded at more competitive universities for subjects judged to be vocational, or if grades are below a specified level. You would need to supply official or certified copies of all academic records and achievements, with a course-by-course evaluation, so that transfer credit can be awarded where appropriate – companies accredited to do this are listed in Chapter 4 (see 'Evaluation of your qualifications'). You would have to make individual enquiries about this as some institutions may do their own evaluation, which would simplify the process. You would also have to take the SAT or ACT tests, and may have to take freshman courses in any required subject areas that you have not studied since GCSE/ Standard grade level. It is also possible to change to another university within the United States, but you would obviously have to go through various formalities with regard to your I-20 form (which is your proof of permission to study only at the institution for which it was issued) and renewing your visa, and pay the associated costs. Permission is only likely to be given to students with a good academic record.

If you already have a first degree, you may find it difficult to gain acceptance as a freshman at some universities or for some courses, and should make early enquiries about this.

It is also possible to transfer to a university in Canada if you have a minimum of one year's post-18 education and meet the criteria, which varies across the country.

Luke is an unusual case as, although a British subject, he has done only two years of his schooling in the UK. Despite the fact that he has been living in the United States for a large part of his life he is considered to be an international student as he does not have US resident status and is on an F-1 visa, which is the type of visa issued to full-time international students. His situation is complicated and he would almost certainly be classed as a foreign student in the UK as well. Luke is also an example of a transfer student as he changed universities after one semester.

I was born in Chiswick and then lived in Hong Kong, the Bahamas and West Palm Beach in Florida as my father was working abroad. We returned to the UK when I was 12 years old and I attended Devonport High School in Plymouth for two years, before returning to West Palm Beach to start my freshman year in high school. I found that I was ahead in sciences, Maths and French and no longer did Latin, which I had studied in England. I did get the opportunity to participate in a business magnet programme and that taught me a lot of business skills that I probably would not have learned in England. I also took Advanced Placement exams, which are relatively new and a good addition to your high school transcript. It was a very natural choice for me to apply to universities in the US and the application procedure was straightforward as I already had a high school GPA and could take the SATs at school. The difference for me was that I had to apply as an international student even though my father was working here. This meant that I had to apply through the US Embassy in London for an F-1 visa and go through the procedure of an interview and providing proof of sufficient funds whilst I was studying here. It also meant that I had to pay international student fees even though I was at high school in Florida. I also have the same work restrictions as all international students.

Although I applied to several universities I decided on FAU (Florida Atlantic University) because it was close to where I was living and had links with the Scripps Institute, a branch of which had recently been established in Florida. As I hope to enter medical school eventually this seemed to be the right choice. I soon found that it was not as it was a new school at the time with very few students and I didn't have the opportunity to play lacrosse, which I really missed. During my first semester there I applied for a transfer to Florida State University. As an international student this meant that I had to sort out my visa status as the permission to study and my SEVIS I-20 form allowed me to study only at the university specified. It took some time to sort this out but I was accepted at FSU, issued with a new I-20 form and am now in the second semester of my sophomore year. It was a good move for me as the campus is much larger and I feel much more at home here. Although a large school the campus is more compact than some and you are always bumping into people you know. I'm now able to play lacrosse and this has made a big difference to my life. I thought about joining a fraternity but I decided I didn't really need to as the lacrosse team is my fraternity – being a team member helps you make lots of friends.

41

My family and I are now in the process of applying for permanent resident status, but this can take some time. It is crucial for me as I plan to major in Biology and then apply to medical school, which is difficult without a green card. I realise that in the UK I would have gone straight to medical school from high school but that is not possible here. I plan to minor in business and feel that this, together with my high school experience, will stand me in good stead if I run a medical practice.

TIP

- Check with the International Center to see whether you can apply for international student tuition waiver. I discovered that I could do this after being at FSU for a semester and now I pay the same fees as Florida residents. This is subject to maintaining a good GPA and I have to re-apply each semester but it's a big help financially.

Luke McHugh, Sophomore
FSU (www.fsu.edu)

04 Applying to universities and colleges

How do I apply?

You can apply to as many institutions as you wish, but should remember that there is a non-returnable fee (usually between $30 and $75) for every application submitted, so it is sensible to research your options thoroughly. There is no national application system like UCAS, and each application must be sent directly to each university you wish to be considered for, using the institution's own form, or the Common Application Form if appropriate. You may, of course, copy the same general information to all institutions, but must take care to note any specific requirements. It is a good idea to get someone (such as parents or teachers) to check everything before you send it off and to ask someone to read through your personal statement or essays. The US Educational Advisory Service offers this service and it is probably worth paying for this (see Appendix 2) if you do not have anyone else who is willing, or feels able, to do it. Current British students have found the service very useful.

Applications for undergraduate courses are made to the Office of Undergraduate Admissions of each institution you apply to, in the majority of cases. Since students do not specialise until the third (junior) year, individual faculties or departments are not normally involved in the initial stage. It is important to note, however, that there are some highly specialised and competitive undergraduate courses which follow a different curriculum and application procedure. An example of this type of limited access programme is in the School of Motion Picture, Television and Recording Arts at Florida State University. Approximately 15 freshmen and 15 transfer students are admitted as film students each year, and applicants must submit the usual application form, a separate application form to the school and a 500–1,000 word essay, in addition to all the other requirements. Another example is the Creative Studies course at UCSB (University of California at Santa Barbara), where students follow a certain amount of independent study and must submit a separate additional application to the College of Creative

Studies. In some cases videos will be required. You must look very carefully at all the requirements when submitting applications.

When do I apply?

It is important to start the application process early – at least one year in advance, which means that your research should ideally start 18 months in advance, as recommended by the EAS. Universities have different closing dates, and the most competitive will usually require earlier applications. Many of the publications and websites mentioned at the end of this book can help you with this process, but it is most important to follow the procedures laid down by the institutions to which you wish to apply. These are described in detail on websites, but make sure you follow the guidelines for international students as these will be different. You will need to make direct contact with institutions at an early stage. The US postal service can be very slow and you may wish to use FedEx or a similar service to make certain that everything arrives by the stated date.

Early Action (EA) and Early Decision (ED)

If you are quite certain that you wish to attend a particular institution you can opt to make an Early Decision, and this will constitute a commitment to that institution. This option may not be available to international students at some institutions. Early Decision is offered by many universities and students who make an Early Decision must commit to the university well ahead of the usual response date of 1 May. This has an advantage for students with a less strong academic record as they may be more likely to get an offer if they make this early commitment. Applicants who are not US citizens and are applying for financial aid might not be considered under the Early Decision option as it does not give them the opportunity to weigh up and compare financial aid packages offered by different universities.

If you have a strong academic record universities may agree to give you a decision much earlier than usual and before your final grades are known under the Early Action programme, which is different from Early Decision and does not commit you to that institution. Harvard no longer offers these options as it was considered to give an unfair advantage to some applicants and there is now a single application deadline of 1 January. These programmes are subject to change at any time and are not necessarily legally binding.

The usual entry requirements

- Your completed application form and accompanying fee.
- Personal statements (also sometimes referred to as 'essays') – including information on extra-curricular achievements. These are likely to be part of the application form.

- Transcripts and certificates showing and explaining your qualifications.
- Reference letters and school reports – these may be part of the application form.
- Test results (SAT or ACT) – these are sent directly by test centres, but you must ensure you take the test(s) required by the dates specified.
- Essays (see below) may be required for some subjects.
- Certification of Financial Responsibility, to show that you will be financed for your course.
- A specified level in the TOEFL if your first language is not English and you have not been educated in a British school.
- Proof of completion of a high-school education or equivalent – this means that you will normally be expected to have been in full-time education until the age of 18.

Interviews and auditions

Because you are usually admitted to the university and not for a specific major, interviews and auditions are not the norm, but will sometimes be required or offered. This will be made clear on application forms and websites, and usually applies in cases of limited access and perform- ance courses (dance, music, etc.).

The application form

The majority of institutions have their own application form which you can either request by mail or download from websites. There is, however, a Common Application Form currently used by 315 member universities and colleges for admission to their undergraduate courses. Many institutions use this form exclusively and all give it equal consideration to their own form. If you are applying to more than one member college, this gives you the advantage of only having to complete one form, which you can photocopy and send to those colleges. The application form can also be completed online (Common App Online) and sent electronically. The website (www. commonapp.org) lists all member colleges, and also provides information on current availability of freshman places, advising whether there are many places, a limited number or none. Remember that you do not specialise in a major subject for the first two years, so place availability is not subject related as in the UK. The website also gives instructions on completing the form and lists frequently asked questions, including essay topics for member colleges. The Common Application Form is posted on the website early in July of the year prior to desired entry and removed early in June of the year of commencement. Please check websites carefully as some participating colleges also require a Common Application Supplement to be submitted at the same time. There is also a Common Application Form for students requesting a transfer to one of the 315 member colleges, but this can only be done online.

You should note that separate applications may be required for specific courses (e.g. Stanford has a separate form for students gifted in art, dance, drama and music, and these students can include materials and opt for an audition).

As with all application forms, it is very important to read the entire form before attempting to complete it, and to follow the instructions carefully. You must pay close attention to closing dates, including the dates by which SAT or ACT scores need to be submitted. A registration fee is required and this must be sent with the application in $US – credit cards will usually be accepted, but otherwise a money order should be sent, unless you have a bank account in the United States. The fee is not refundable.

■ Essays and personal statements

Essays and personal statements may be an integral part of the application form. Essays can refer to a statement you are asked to write about yourself and, in this respect, are similar to the Personal Statement required on UCAS forms in the UK. Some American universities are now using the term 'personal statement' on the application form. Many universities, however, also set or use standard essay topics to show that you have thought about an issue and can explain your views and how you reached them.

The personal statement type of essay is very important in applications to American universities, most of which stress the importance of qualities such as leadership, community service and evidence of non-academic interests. Admissions staff frequently stress that they take the 'holistic' approach and look for well-rounded students. Some university websites give quite a bit of advice on this and it is worth looking at these before submitting your application. In addition to academic excellence, many top universities look for students who have made a significant commitment to any single non-academic area, such as athletics, music, art, leadership or community service, as well as those who have pursued a wide variety of activities.

The other type of essay commonly requested looks for an ability to think about an issue and put forward a logical, reasoned argument. This is becoming a more significant part of the selection procedure with its inclusion in the new SAT, as described later in this chapter. This type of essay will require you to take a position on an issue, and use examples to support the position you have taken. Essays are already part of the application procedure in those institutions using the Common Application Form, and you will be able to submit the same one to all those you apply to within this group. Essay topics are given on www.commonapp.org and include the option of a topic of your choice. Popular topics include the discussion of an issue of personal, national or international concern; the evaluation of a significant experience or achievement or ethical dilemma; a description of someone who has had a significant influence on you; or of a fictional or historical character or significant work or discovery which has influenced or impressed you. You would normally be expected to write between 250 and 500 words. If you are asked to fit your essay into a clearly defined space on the application form you should not exceed this. You may be asked to write on the application form and send a computer-generated copy, to make it easier for admissions staff to read.

■ Transcripts of your qualifications

Your academic record is known as a 'transcript' in the United States, and evidence of this will always be required. Sometimes the original certificates you have gained in secondary school will be sufficient, and you may be asked to send copies with your application and bring the original certificates with you if you take up a place. Although many institutions are familiar with the more traditional British qualifications, they may still request copies of syllabuses of the work you have covered, in addition to proof of your grades. Academic records should be sent directly from your school or college, with an official seal or signed statement. Any transcripts you submit yourself will not be considered official, although you are entitled to offer an explanation of a course if you feel that this will enhance your application. The institution(s) you are applying to will make their requirements clear, and you can check them on their websites by selecting the information for freshman and international applications. If an institution is not familiar with your qualifications, they may ask you to have these evaluated by an independent organisation, and you will have to pay for this. Some larger institutions, including the University of California (all campuses), have specialists who are very familiar with AS and A levels, and will evaluate and make offers on these at no cost to the student. The specialists at the various campuses work closely together to ensure they are making consistent judgements, as they may not be familiar with more recently introduced subjects.

Universities will be interested in the syllabus as well as the grades obtained, and will not necessarily give all subjects equal weighting. Although it may be possible to receive some credits for areas of work already covered at an advanced level, the broad nature of the courses for the freshman and sophomore years means that there will still be quite a number of subjects you are not familiar with, and you may be required to study some subjects you left behind after GCSE or equivalent.

If you have taken a less well-known qualification such as a BTEC National Diploma, you will almost certainly have to submit transcripts for evaluation, regardless of whether you wish to apply for credits, and you can expect to pay for this.

As has already been stated, the IB is widely accepted, and credits are awarded on receipt of proof of your grades for the subjects taken.

Evaluation of your qualifications

If you wish to claim credits during your freshman year, or to transfer from another higher education or professional course, you may need to pay to have your qualifications evaluated by a recognised private company. You should clarify this when applying. If your qualifications need to be evaluated by a recognised private agency, the university considering your admission will supply the necessary forms. Services recommended by American universities include:

- AACRAO (American Association of Collegiate Registrars and Admissions Officers) Credential Evaluation Service, One Dupont Circle, NW, Suite 520, Washington, DC 20036, USA. Email: oies@aacrao.org; Website: www.aacrao.org.
- Josef Silny & Associates, PO Box 248233, Coral Gables, FL 33124, USA. Email: info@silny.com; Website: www.jsilny.com.
- Educational Credential Evaluators, Inc., PO Box 514070, Milwaukee, WI 53203–3470, USA. Email: eval@ece.org; Website: www.ece.org.
- World Education Services, Inc., PO Box 745, Old Chelsea Station, New York, NY 10113–0745, USA. Email: info@wes.org; Website: www.wes.org.

Two Harvard students recount their experiences

I first became interested in applying to American universities after reading a newspaper article which showed several American universities listed in the world's top 10 rankings alongside Oxford and Cambridge. I was at this time considering where I would like to apply to study after taking my A levels and the article gave me the idea of looking at what American universities had to offer.

After looking at the websites of several American universities I found that the main difference between the UK and the American system was that you were encouraged to take a wider range of courses to make up your degree rather than just specialising in one subject. This appealed to me and after attending a College Open day in London hosted by the Fulbright Commission I decided to apply to MIT and Harvard as well as Cambridge University. The College Open day was an ideal opportunity to speak to representatives from many American universities and attend talks on the application process.

I was the first person from my state school in Wootton, Bedford-shire to apply to an Ivy League university so they had no experience of the application process. They were extremely supportive of my decision to apply and were happy to help me with the application and complete all the references that were required.

I spent a lot of time looking at the websites of Harvard and MIT. Both had a considerable amount of information about the application process for international students. The only difficulty I had was in understanding some of the terms that are not used in the UK. As you are required to take SAT tests, I used the College Board website to get information on the tests I was required to take and to book my tests in the UK.

As part of my application I was asked to attend an interview for MIT in Cambridge, England and an interview for Harvard in London. Both interviews were relaxed and at both I was asked about my interests as well as what I was doing academically.

I was lucky enough to have offers from Cambridge University, MIT and Harvard. I was already familiar with Cambridge University and had visited there several times previously. I had never visited MIT or Harvard, so I used the visiting weekends they hold in April to have a look round and meet others that would be joining the same class. Both weekends were busy but they gave me an ideal opportunity to see what MIT and Harvard had to offer and what it would be like to study in America. Both universities had excellent facilities and I would have been happy to study at either institution. I finally made the decision to accept the offer from Harvard.

The visa application process was started by Harvard, who sent me an I-20 form and instruction sheet. I used the American Embassy website to complete several forms online and make payments for the application and then made an appointment for the interview. I had to show that I would be financially supported during my time in the US. I receive need-based financial assistance from Harvard and an additional contribution from my parents and had to provide proof of this.

I found settling into Harvard relatively easy. I had been given the names of my room-mates a few weeks before starting so had been in contact with them before leaving the UK. Harvard also runs an international students' week before the American students arrive. This was a great opportunity to meet other international students and we were given advice on setting up bank accounts and getting mobile phones.

I have found that in the US students are tested far more frequently and homework seems to account for a significant amount of the grade. Each of my years at Harvard has equal weighting so there is less pressure in the last year, but you have to be prepared to *work hard in your first year. I plan to major in Physics. As well as studying most students participate in sports and other activities and I have joined the swim team.*

**Aaron Deardon, Freshman
(www.harvard.edu)**

I didn't apply to universities in the UK because I wanted academic flexibility and the opportunity to explore other areas of interest and pursue my sporting interests. I have been a keen tennis player for many years, represented my county throughout my career and played at national level. Here at Harvard I'm on the varsity team.

I went to Sevenoaks School, an independent co-ed, and took the IB instead of A levels. I took Spanish, English and Biology at higher level and Italian, Maths and Philosophy at standard level, gaining high grades across the board. The IB offers a much broader education than A levels and that fits well with the US system.

My school careers service helped me to find out about the opportunities and I also used websites and a guide called 'The Top 100 colleges in the US'. The deciding factor for me was my visit to the campus and I would strongly advise anyone to visit the universities they are considering applying to. There is a certain intangible feeling to each place, and it's important to find the right one for you. I visited during the previous summer, and was interviewed on campus. I got a great feel for the place, and then applied Early Action* and was successful! I also had an interview in London during the application process. Financial aid here is available but based on need. I didn't apply so my family pays the $45,000 a year that it costs to study here. I had to provide proof of that to get my student visa.

I can study a wide range of subjects here but my main area of interest is literature and this will be my major. My current study incorporates English, Philosophy, Spanish and some film/visual art studies.

I think the breadth and flexibility of academic subject matter studied is one of the main advantages here. Others are the outstanding extra-curricular opportunities and sports facilities. The resources and ease of getting funds to pursue research and other areas of interest are unrivalled at Harvard. If you prefer early specialisation and the intense study of one area of study from the beginning then the UK would have the advantage. I think there would also be more free time to foster creativity.

---

* At some universities you can choose to apply Early Action (EA) as long as you submit your application early, together with test scores and other requirements (see page 44).

*There are many opportunities for extra-curricular activities in
the US and I continued my involvement with charity work that
had started during my school years. Many college students are
involved with NGO work and my particular thing is the Circle of
Women (www.circleofwomen.org), which is run by Harvard women
undergraduates and promotes education in developing countries,
specifically for women and girls.*

*Although I recognise that there is a big culture difference
between English (or 'commonwealth') people and Americans,
I didn't really have a problem adapting to life as an American
student. I have absolutely no regrets about my decision and am
having a wonderful experience!*

TIPS

- *It's important to think about the application process early – there's
  a lot of information to absorb and forms to complete and if rushing
  it, it is too much to handle. Don't be intimidated by the prospect!
  Although there was no real difficulty in taking the SAT or getting the
  F-1 visa the administrative hassle is considerable in both cases.*
- *Make use of the US Educational Advisory Service at the Fulbright
  Commission (for details see Appendix 2) as the information
  and advice they can offer is invaluable – if it's not possible to
  visit personally you can email your questions to an adviser. The
  library is very comprehensive.*
- *You will feel homesick at first, but stick it out and you will be
  rewarded. Most people are homesick for the first few weeks
  or even months – talk to your parents and friends, or the
  counsellors who are there to help you.*

**Elizabeth Brook, Sophomore
(www.harvard.edu)**

■ The SAT and ACT tests

There has been quite a bit of discussion about the tests used for admission to undergraduate courses in the United States as they tend to test potential rather than achievement, and rely significantly on multiple-choice questions. They are used in conjunction with knowledge-based qualifications and are required by the majority of American universities, although there is a campaign to change this practice (see www.fairtest.org/ – the website of the National Center for Fair and Open Testing in Cambridge, Massachusetts).

The website carries a list of some 755 colleges apparently not using the tests for selection purposes, but you must check with the institutions directly as they may still require you to take them (e.g. the California State system – different from the University of California campuses). If you check the list of colleges on this website, you will notice that there are qualifying footnotes against many of them. Some require only out-of-state applicants to take the tests, some require them only when the minimum GPA and class ranking are not met, some require only SAT subject tests and some use them only for placement and academic advice purposes. It is also worth noting that many of the institutions on this list are specialist colleges, including those for art and music, and they may see the tests as less relevant. Most students will find that they do need to take these tests if they want to keep a range of options open. Almost all major institutions still require them and they are never a disadvantage.

Some research has suggested that there is no correlation between SAT Reasoning test scores and academic achievement, and it has been suggested that males tend to score better in them than females of similar ability. Mount Holyoke College, a women's college in Massachusetts, and Sarah Lawrence, a liberal arts college in New York City, no longer require SAT or ACT scores. Other colleges have made, or may be about to make, similar announcements, but these are definitely in the minority, and many universities will not even consider applicants without SAT or ACT scores. You should take the SAT if you have a choice as it will be accepted everywhere and the ACT has been designed for students following a US curriculum. Some students take both.

It is widely recognised that scores can be improved by 10 to 20 per cent with coaching, and practice papers are widely available in paper or electronic format. You should aim to get as much information about them as possible and do the practice papers. You can re-take SAT tests, but all scores are reported. There are UK-based companies and individuals offering test preparation courses, mainly for the SAT, Graduate Record Examination (GRE) and Graduate Management Admissions Test (GMAT). Details of these can be obtained from www.fulbright.co.uk.

A fee is payable for all tests.

SAT Reasoning test

This is designed as a measure of critical thinking, analytical and problem-solving skills in critical reading, writing and Maths. Each section is scored on a scale of 200–800 and administered six times a year overseas. You can find out more about the types of questions by visiting the SAT Preparation Center at www.collegeboard.com.

At the most competitive universities, the majority of students currently achieve a combined score of more than 1340, and a score of 1010 or above will normally be expected at all competitive institutions.

SAT subject tests

These are designed to measure your knowledge and skills in particular subject areas and two or three of these are frequently required in addition to the SAT Reasoning test at the more selective institutions. All are one-hour multiple-choice tests and independent of any particular textbook. Some colleges specify subjects whilst others leave the choice to applicants. Some specify that students who have taken the Advanced Placement examinations or the IB will not have to take SAT subject tests. This may also apply to A levels and Advanced Highers, but you would need to ask about this. Academic subject tests are offered in Literature, US History, World History, Maths, Biology, Chemistry, Physics, Chinese, French, German, Modern Hebrew, Italian, Japanese, Korean, Latin and Spanish.

The ACT test

This is designed to assess general educational development and ability to complete college-level work. It consists of multiple-choice tests in the four skill areas of English, Maths, reading and science.

There is also an optional writing test, which many major universities require of students offering only the ACT test. Although universities will accept the SAT or ACT, many require some SAT subject tests as well.

At the most selective universities, the majority of students will have an ACT score of over 29 and scores of 18 or above will normally be expected at all competitive universities.

■ Taking the SAT or ACT tests

Check with the institutions you are applying to early – what tests do they require you to take and when do the results have to reach them?

Information on registration, fees, test centres and registration forms can be obtained from the EAS at the Fulbright Commission in London (see Appendix 2). The SAT test is given in the UK six times a year, and you should pre-register at least six weeks in advance of the registration date. You should aim to take the test in the autumn before you wish to be admitted to university. Most UK-based students take the SAT at the American School in London, but there are other centres for those living in other parts of the country. You *cannot* just turn up on the day. You will need to supply the SAT or ACT Institutional Codes for the universities you are applying to, so that your scores can be sent to them. These codes can be found in the admissions information literature.

Contact details

Arrangements to take the SAT in the UK can also be made with The Educational Testing Service – UK office, 707 High Road, London, N12 0BT: Email: contact-uk@etseurope.org; Tel: 0208 446 9944 (www.ets.org). The easiest thing is to register online and pay by credit card: www.collegeboard.com.

For information on the ACT, contact the EAS at the Fulbright Commission or visit www.act.org.

You can only register for the test online and there are currently four test centres in the UK.

Special services are available for students with disabilities.

■ Letters of recommendation (references)

Most universities will ask for two or three letters of recommendation, including at least one from the student's school or college. Typically, an American student will be asked to submit a reference from the high-school counsellor, but it is recognised that the British system is different and you are likely to be asked for a reference from the head or principal of your school or college. If three references are required, the other two could be from two different subject teachers or one teacher and a careers or personal adviser, community worker or employer, to outline any voluntary work or particular skills you have acquired. The letter of recommendation does not necessarily indicate a separate letter, as there may be a space for references on the application form in the same way as the UCAS system.

■ English language tests

If your native language is not English and you have not studied in an English-speaking country for at least one year, you will be required to provide evidence of having achieved a minimum standard, and your official test scores will have to be sent to those institutions you apply to. In the TOEFL tests, which are universally accepted, the usual minimum score is 550 for the paper-based examination, or 213 for the computer-based test. An internet-based test (TOEFL iBT) is available worldwide and is said to provide better information about students' ability to communicate in an academic setting and their readiness for academic work. Further information, including dates and locations for UK tests and practice tests, can be found on the ETS website (www.ets.org). Many universities also accept the International English Language Testing System (IELTS) with a score of seven (www.ielts.org). Some universities may require students to take their own English as a Second Language examination and, in some cases, require further study before starting the course.

Canada

■ Applying to Canadian universities and colleges

This application procedure varies from province to province. In Ontario applications are through the Ontario Universities Application Centre (OUAC). This also includes colleges such as the Ontario College of Art and Design (OCAD) which is Canada's largest art college and located in the heart of Toronto. International students complete the OUAC 105F (international) application online and can make three choices. You can pay by credit card – the basic fee is CAN $110 + $10 for mailing addresses outside Canada with additional fees for further choices, transcript requests or for paying by cheque. Many universities in Ontario require additional evaluation fees and these are paid directly to the university. They are usually between $40 and $60 but can be higher. Direct application is made to colleges outside the OUAC system.

British Columbia also has a central admissions service called the Post-secondary Application Service of British Columbia (PASBC) (www.bccampus.ca) which accepts applications for all post-secondary institutions. This is a free service and you pay only the cost of application charged by the institution(s) you are applying to. You complete a common form with your personal details and an institutional application form with details of the place and course you are applying for. You can use the common form for several institutions. You can also apply directly to some universities and will need to check individual websites for guidance.

In most provinces applications are made directly to the university and this can usually be done online. You will need to check the websites of the institutions you are considering applying to for further details. You will find a section dedicated to international students and this will have details of how to apply and pay the fee. Major credit cards are usually accepted and costs are usually around Canadian $100.

Students who have not been educated in English must pass an English test, but there is no French test that international students are required to pass for admission to a French-language institution. Each institution will assess the level of proficiency.

Entry requirements for British students are similar to those required in the UK and were described in the last chapter. You will need to supply evidence of these – either school-certified copies of results sent in a sealed institution envelope or you can arrange for them to be sent direct from examination boards. Universities may still require you to present the originals when you arrive. Your school will need to provide a reference and predicted grades of any examinations not yet taken and you will be expected to provide a personal statement, which is likely to be part of the application form. Some institutions also require an essay – details can be found on websites. No other tests are normally required.

For art and design colleges you will normally have to mail a port-folio of your work if you are unable to attend an interview. At OCAD, for example, you are not required to present your portfolio in person if you live more than 800 kilometres from Toronto.

Auditions will normally be required for drama, dance and music courses as in the UK. Entry to the top colleges is very competitive. The National Theatre School of Canada, a private school in Montreal, auditions over 1,000 prospective students annually for the acting course and accepts only 12 of these. International students are not eligible for the grants and loans available to Canadian citizens and residents and the fees are currently $8,400 per annum, which is double that for Canadians.

Apply early – preferably at least eight months in advance even if a later closing date is specified.

Students from American high schools are usually required to have taken the SAT, but it is not necessary for applicants from the UK as GCE A and AS levels, Scottish Highers/Advanced Highers and the IB are well recognised at major universities.

05 Financing your study

United States

■ Certification of financial responsibility

The cost of your undergraduate course is a very important consideration, and it is your responsibility to ensure that you are financially prepared for the entire course. In most cases, parents or a relative will be taking on this responsibility, with supplementary money from summer vacation employment in the UK and any work you manage to obtain on campus. Universities are required by federal law to verify the financial resources of each applicant prior to issuing the Certificate of Eligibility (Form I-20 or IAP-66). You must complete the Certification of Financial Responsibility and submit it along with proof of financial support, which could be bank statements, award letters, scholarships or other acceptable evidence. You must show proof of financial support for the first year of study and demonstrate availability of funds for the entire course.

You should plan for a 10 per cent annual increase in the cost of tuition fees, room and board and other costs, including books and insurance. Undergraduates in the United States typically spend more on books as there is usually a required reading list for each credit, and most students take four credit courses per semester. Married students will be required to show evidence of funding to support an accompanying spouse and any children.

Annual tuition fees vary from around $9,000 (rare) to $35,000 or higher. The average for a top competitive institution is currently around $30,000, and for a good public-sector college $18,000 (although American citizens who attend public universities in their home state will typically pay considerably less). The cost of room and board also varies according to the location and you can expect to pay between $7,000 and $14,000 per annum. Books and insurance are likely to cost a further $1,500, and you must allow at least $2,000 for miscellaneous costs. You cannot enrol at an American university without full medical insurance and, in many cases, you will be required to participate in the university's own health insurance plan – this will be at a favourable rate and is clearly to your advantage. Most institutions have excellent student health services.

You are, therefore, likely to be asked to provide proof that you have funds of at least $27,000 per year and, in many cases, considerably more than this. Stanford advises a figure of nearly $50,000 per year, Harvard $47,215 and UCLA $45,000. Information and guidelines can be found on websites or obtained directly from any university to which you are considering applying. Remember that the cost of living is very high in cities such as New York, Boston, Los Angeles and San Francisco.

Scholarships

A small number of scholarships are available to international students at American universities, but the majority are restricted to American citizens. The policy varies from university to university, as does the amount available. Private institutions with large endowments and wealthy alumni can typically offer financial assistance to a much larger number of students, and can choose how they distribute these funds. Harvard awards a large number of scholarships (more than 50 per cent of students receive some needs-based assistance), but it is extremely difficult to obtain a place there. Both Harvard and Stanford universities have very large endowments and announced in 2008 that tuition fees will be waived to all students admitted whose families earn below a specified amount and also room and board fees for those earning even lower amounts. Stanford has set the second figure at $60,000 a year and these students will have neither tuition nor room and board costs. Those whose families earn less then $100,000 will receive free tuition. At Harvard those whose family income is below $60,000 will pay nothing, between $60,000 and $120,000 the cost will be on a sliding scale from 0 to 10 per cent and between $120,000 and $180,000 it will be 10 per cent of income. Other selective universities with good endowments are also offering tuition waiver – MIT, for example, will provide free tuition to students whose family income is below $75,000. These figures are subject to change and you will need to check them.

The total cost to attend many prestigious private institutions is between $45,000 and $50,000 and the awards tend to represent a significant proportion of this. These institutions are looking for the most able students and are prepared to fund them to a high level if they need it. Other institutions awarding more scholarships offer a smaller percentage of the total cost. It is worth remembering that the trend is now to offer scholarships on the basis of need rather than merit. In other words, institutions will select the students they want without any reference to need and then fund those from lower-income families. You are advised to be wary of services offering to find scholarships for a fee.

You must submit an International Student Financial Aid Application form which colleges will provide.

The student in the following case study came to the US on an academic scholarship.

Although my family was living in the UK I had been at a boarding school out of the country for a few years so my case is a bit unusual. My mother is a single parent and I thought that I might not be eligible for home fees in the UK so I looked at options in the US as a fail-safe measure. I had also had the opportunity to visit MIT as part of an exchange programme a year earlier, although I did not know at the time that I could apply. I did, however, get home status and applied through UCAS and got unconditional offers from Manchester, Leeds and Liverpool universities as well as my desired choice of Sheffield University. Due to financial constraints I was unable to attend interviews in England and for that reason I lost my place in the Cambridge application process.

I used the College Board website and talked to alumni at my high school to find out about American universities and my high school arranged for me to take the SAT tests.

My final choice was really made on economic grounds as I wanted to put the least amount of pressure on my mother. MIT offered a great scholarship with a family contribution of only $2,750. However, I'm currently on a full scholarship. Furthermore, after four years I worked out that I would owe MIT only $16,000 with comfortable methods to pay this off. In England, on the other hand, the higher cost of housing and general living conditions would build up a debt of more than £16,000 in the same time. As the child of a single mother with a brother I believe I made the best decision for all of us in choosing MIT. It didn't seem so easy to apply for financial help in England. I also had international friends and the US was much more welcoming and therefore more of a viable option for me.

I experienced no difficulties in getting my visa as the personnel at the US Embassy in England and MIT made the F-1 process extremely fast. I had the scholarship from MIT and a loan if needed and that provided the required proof of my financial security. MIT has secured housing on campus for all four years so I have no accommodation problems either.

Although I am currently taking a wide range of subjects my main area of study is Aeronautics and Astronautics and I plan to major in this area. UK higher education is much narrower than in the US, focusing more on what one will end up doing. However US higher education takes a general approach before focusing on the major.

Due to the current exchange rate US education and living costs can be cheaper than in the UK and it seems to me that there are more funds allocated for needy students in the US than in the UK. I do not regret my decision since I believe it would have been more detrimental to my growth after graduation owing so much more in the UK than I will owe to MIT.

Nana Essilfie-Conduah, Freshman
MIT
(www.mit.edu)

Athletics scholarships

Athletics scholarships are different as the coach for each sport has a great deal of power in deciding where the scholarships will go, and will simply be looking for the best athletes who can also meet the minimum academic standards. Competitive sport is much more important in the American higher education system, where it is often a major part of the social life in the surrounding area as well as on campus. Games are televised, and hotel rooms are usually full when an important match is played between rival football (American), baseball and basketball teams.

The NCAA (National Collegiate Athletic Association) has three divisions and over 900 universities who are full members. The standard required for a scholarship is extremely high, and many students have gone on to become top international athletes. Only students with the very highest standard are likely to be recruited at this level, and most will have competed in national teams. They cannot, however, have professional status. There are athletics associations for smaller colleges where scholarships may be available and the standard will not be so high. The amount of the scholarship varies from a few thousand dollars to over $30,000 per year for a full scholarship.

It is important to make early contact with the athletic directors or coaches at institutions to which you wish to apply. It is often possible to make an initial contact with them at international meetings if you are participating at this level. Alternatively, you can obtain the contact details from websites (e.g. the NCAA site at www.ncaa.org) or publications, and send in your CV (resumé) and a videotape. Some coaches will actively recruit the top athletes, but you should also actively seek out the opportunities yourself if you fulfil the criteria. There is an NCAA clearing house for which a fee is payable.

There is a limit to the number of scholarships which can be awarded in each sport and a federal law which requires that an equal amount of funding must be given to males and females. This could give an advantage to females since many sports scholars in the United States are footballers – the football played in Europe is known as soccer in the United States, and there will also be scholarships for this.

The student in the following case study started off on an athletics scholarship.

I first thought about studying in America after talking to people I met on the tennis circuit. I went to a state high school in Cambridge and played tennis at county and national level so most of my weekends were taken up with this. I had never been to the US and never in a million years would I have thought about going to university there. With the encouragement of my brother, however, I found out more about the opportunities offered to athletes at American universities and was attracted to the idea of being able to continue to develop as a tennis player and get a degree at the same time. I was introduced to a company started by two former tennis scholars and specialising in matching players to American universities offering scholarships. I had already applied to universities through UCAS and was a late applicant to the US system. My place at the University of Houston was not finalised until April, but I was lucky and they offered me an athletics scholarship. I would like to stress that the earlier on in the academic year you decide you want to study in the US on a sports scholarship the better as coaches like to recruit players early and fill their available scholarships as soon as possible. Therefore you will get more offers and have more time to decide and do your research than I did. This is especially true for guys looking for sports scholarships as it is much more difficult to get 100% scholarships compared to women because of title IX ruling (this law was implemented to ensure equality for males and females and there is a lot more competition for American football scholarships than for other sports) on gender equality.

Although things worked out well for me in the end I wish I had done more initial research and thought more about the cultural differences in other parts of the US. I would probably have been more attracted to the north east of the US from the cultural point of view, but I do realise that there are bigger all-round sporting universities in the south where sports scholars are treated as professional athletes.

As you do a broad range of studies for the first two years and then choose your major subject it was a bit like doing my GCSEs again to begin with. I completed the first two years at Houston and then my coach decided to move to Florida State University in Tallahassee. As I had a good relationship with her and knew that the level of tennis was higher I decided to request a transfer for my final two years and moved here to complete my studies, majoring in Exercise Science. I was lucky that the two universities play in different 'conferences' as there are NCAA (National Collegiate Athletics Association) rules about transferring within the same group. My tennis did not fare so well here, partly due to the higher level and partly due to an injury for which surgery was recommended. The cost was fully covered. My scholarship did not transfer with me but my parents agreed to support me financially during my junior year. It was a difficult first year and there were times when I was ready to pack up and go home, but I am very glad that I stuck it out as it has been a great experience for me overall. One of the problems was that I entered a new institution as a junior and wasn't aware of all the procedures so I found some courses I wanted to take were already full. I knew that I needed the twelve credit hours to maintain my visa status and had to persuade tutors to register me. It's vital to register early for courses as they can fill up very quickly. In a big institution you have to be prepared to ask and often have to find out things for yourself. I wasn't aware, for example that I could have followed an honours curriculum as I had a good grade point average. I don't really regret that as a dissertation is required and that's quite a time-commitment.

After the injury I took a year off competitive tennis. I was still a team member and was fortunate enough to be able to practice and travel with the team, but was not allowed to compete in collegiate matches. This helped a lot with my recovery as being in a team is like being part of a family. I never felt the need to join a sorority and have never even been curious enough to find out more about them – they simply don't appeal to me. My senior year was by far my best as the women's tennis team set new records for FSU and I got my degree. I knew by this time that I would not succeed as a professional tennis player, but I love all sports and know I want to be involved with athletics. I can analyse a fellow player's game and give advice, but I have been less successful at applying this to my own game.

As I didn't feel that I had enough experience or training to find the kind of job I'd like to do I decided to apply for a second degree and am now majoring in Athletic Training, which is in the school of nutrition, food and exercise science. I didn't have to repeat the freshman and sophomore years and was able to get straight into the theoretical and clinical training. Every afternoon is spent working with FSU athletes in rehabilitation, concentrating on injury prevention and treatment. We use various machines in the same way as a physiotherapist might but concentrate on sports injuries. At the moment I have to work under supervision but can take a national certification examination along with my degree. The course suits me very well as I am the kind of person who learns best when I have the chance to apply the theory. Even though I'm no longer in the tennis team I still get some financial help from athletics and also qualified for tuition waiver so that I pay in-state fees. I earn some money coaching as well.

My next step will probably be to take up the opportunity to do optional practical training so that I can earn some money and gain relevant experience. After this I am thinking about an MA in Athletic Training and am looking at other universities, including the University of Georgia in Athens. I was lucky in that I got the chance to visit a lot of campuses when playing in the tennis team. I think that I will have an advantage when looking for work in athletic training as I have the experience of having been an athlete to add to my qualifications.

I am now on my second F-1 student visa and there was no problem in getting this renewed. I must stress that it is important to understand and follow the rules. At first I thought the visa was enough but you must also have a valid I-20 form or you could be sent back. You have to get this signed every time you leave the country. When I got my new visa I didn't realise that you cannot enter the US more than 30 days before the start of the new visa and I came 32 days before. I was lucky to get an immigration officer on a good day!

If you come out here on a sports scholarship and get yourself into the right institution to further your ultimate goals in the sport, you will be treated like a professional athlete. These chances are just not available to the same extent in the UK. If you are unsure exactly where to go with your sporting career a US university can be a great stepping stone to see if you can make it. The majority of sports scholars, however, will not become professional athletes so you need to think about alternative careers.

I would advise you to look at all the options before applying and to find out more about the recognition of your qualifications when you return to the UK.

You will find cultural differences here and I think you need to be aware that comments on these can sometimes be offensive. At first I found myself saying 'That's typically American' until my coach cautioned me about this, telling me that I had chosen to come here and should not be so critical. I never do this now!

Miranda Foley, second undergraduate degree
Florida State University
(www.fsu.edu)

The student in the following case study chose to reject scholarships to attend a university with a higher standard of tennis

I am perhaps a bit unusual in that I came to Florida at the age of 13 to attend the Nick Bollettieri Tennis Academy (now known as IMG Academies) in Bradenton. I was a very keen tennis player and had been on summer courses there for a couple of years. It was a big step to take but my parents fully supported me and wanted to give me the chance to develop as a player. We had to attend school of course and I entered the 9th grade of a private high school where

I had normal lessons in the morning and then played tennis from 2:00 to 5:00 pm. At first my parents were back in Bristol most of the time and I lived at the academy, but they bought a house in the area later and my mother spent six months a year there so I could live at home. I have had a normal F-1 student visa from the start and renew it when required. It has never been a problem.

It was tough at first but I got to know a lot of people there and made many friends. It was a unique experience and I had to grow up fast. Despite the intensive training I wasn't offered a scholarship at FSU as the standard here is very high and the competition very keen. I was offered scholarships at other universities where the standard was not so high, but I chose FSU as I did get a place on the team and played professional tournaments at the first level. I didn't do that well and found it tough to work so hard and not get the results so I am no longer on the team. I trained a lot but now feel that I didn't play enough tournaments to compete successfully at this level.

As I was not in a UK high school I applied in the same way as any American student, with my grade point average, school transcripts and SAT score being assessed. I graduated from high school with honours and was accepted at FSU. The difference for me was that my parents were not permanent residents so I didn't qualify for in-state fees. I did quite well academically though so I was soon able to apply to the International Center for tuition waiver and now pay in-state fees.

I was in some ways fortunate as the transition to higher education was very easy for me as I was used to being away from home and used to the education system. I had taken a broad range of subjects throughout high school so I didn't find myself in the position of having to take subjects I hadn't done since the age of 16. In fact it was pretty much like an extended high school education. Although Mathematics has always been a fairly strong subject for me, I became really interested in English Literature and this would probably surprise some of my former teachers. I am majoring in English Literature with minors in Communications and Philosophy and I think it's great to be able to continue to take courses other than your major.

This is my final year and I have loved every minute of it. I have become very used to the American culture and don't really feel that I would be so happy back in England – after all I have lived virtually half my life here. There are cultural differences and I love the atmosphere of a big campus and the way in which American students take pride in their college identity and in wearing clothes which identify their allegiance.

I have not completely decided on the next step, but would like to work in something related to the media or to politics. I am looking around for something now and have approached a few people about taking me on as I am allowed a period of optional practical training. After this I am thinking in terms of an MA, but everything is still quite open for me.

I would certainly encourage other young people who have achieved a good standard in a sport to think about American universities. Sport is big business on the US campus and there are opportunities at various levels. The balance between sport and classes is good in America and done in such a way that the athlete doesn't struggle with trying to cope with both at the same time. I know I didn't make the gains I had hoped to on the tennis court but I don't blame the system for that and I've had a great time and done well in my studies.

TIPS

- *Make use of the International Center or equivalent as they have all the answers to queries about status and forms and are happy to help. Make sure you get them to sign your I-20 form every time you leave the country – you won't normally get back in without it. Don't leave this to the last minute and expect them to drop everything and sign it – take it a couple of weeks in advance.*
- *Once you get a place at a university get in contact with the International Center as you never know what sort of extras they may be able to provide you with (e.g. the out-of-state waiver).*
- *Early application is advisable for all students, regardless of whether they are seeking scholarships. A lot of paper work and an interview at the US Embassy are needed to get your visa so the more time you have the better.*
- *It's vital to register early for courses as they can fill up very quickly.*
- *Do your research thoroughly if you are looking for a scholarship and take advantage of any contacts you make.*

Stefan Shaw, Senior
FSU, Tallahassee

Academic requirements for athletes

There has been a lot of publicity about top athletes, footballers in particular, being admitted without the academic requirements for undergraduate study. This is strongly denied by universities, and there is certainly evidence that many athletes do have strong academic credentials. At the same time, however, it is certainly possible to gain admission to a top academic institution with lower SAT scores and examination grades than would otherwise be required. You must not assume, however, that this is always the case, as many Ivy League universities, including Princeton, give no special financial or academic consideration to the athletes they recruit, on the grounds that the purpose of higher education is to enhance academic training and maturity.

Athletes are naturally expected to compete for the university in addition to their national commitments, and spend many hours training every day. Coaches tend to advise on the academic programme and frequently suggest courses in which students are not required to attend all classes, and which do not involve practical or laboratory work. When athletes are heavily involved in competition or are struggling with a course, coaches may make funds available to pay for additional help.

In addition to the most popular sports already mentioned, a reasonable number of scholarships are available in tennis, gymnastics, soccer, swimming and diving, cross country, golf, field hockey, ice hockey, track and field, softball and volleyball. A very few scholarships are available in sports such as archery, badminton, sailing, equestrian events, fencing, figure skating, skiing, rugby, martial arts, squash and water polo. Most universities will offer only the most popular sports and you will have to search websites for minority sports.

Athletes are allowed to compete for four years, although scholarships are provided on an annual basis. The US Educational Advisory Service at the Fulbright Commission (see Appendix 2) produces a detailed free leaflet on athletic scholarships.

Canada

■ Costs in Canada

The cost of courses at Canadian universities varies between schools and courses. Typically an international student can expect to pay between Canadian $6,000 and $17,000 per year for an undergraduate course. An amount of $8,000– $9,000 for a basic course is about average. In general Manitoba is the cheapest province and British Columbia and Quebec the most expensive, but individual universities in other provinces may be considerably higher than average. At some all courses are over $15,000 a year for international students. You need to check this and the possibility of financial aid. Canadian citizens will pay from $3,500 to $5,000 for undergraduate courses. The province of Quebec subsidises this for its residents and they will pay less.

Living costs differ according to the location, but are likely to be between $4,000 and $5,000 per annum for a room only. You will need to add the cost of books, travel, food, insurance, clothes and entertainment to this. It is estimated that you should budget for around $12,000 living costs per annum although this varies between the provinces and locations.

■ Scholarships and financial help

According to the Association of Universities and Colleges of Canada the number of Canadian universities offering entrance scholarships for international students is growing and you can get information about these from the financial aid offices of the universities you are considering. The major universities all offer some kind of financial assistance, sometimes on merit and sometimes on need. Many of them also offer scholarships for a variety of sports for those who have reached a high level.

CIS (Canadian Interuniversity Sport) is the equivalent of the NCAA in the US and member institutions do provide partial awards to help with living and tuition costs. International students of a high standard may qualify for home tuition fees and/or receive additional awards.

The AUCC also administers some scholarships for international students.

Most students are able to claim the GST/HST (goods and services tax) credit, but must apply for it. Students with families can claim child benefit after 18 months. All the information is on the Canada Revenue Agency website (www.cra-arc.gc.ca/menu-e.html).

■ Health care

Unlike the United States, Canadian provinces do have health care plans but the rules vary from one province to another and international students are not always covered. Health Canada has links to all of the provincial websites (www.hc-sc.gc.ca/hcs-sss/medi-assur/res/links-liens_e.html). Some provinces, notably Alberta, British Columbia, Newfoundland and Saskatchewan cover international students under their provincial health care plans. You may find that you have to enrol in a specified basic health plan for an initial short period before coming under the province's medical services plan. Medical insurance is required when registering for a course. In Nova Scotia cover is available to international students but there's a one-year waiting period, necessitating private health insurance for the first year. Universities usually offer a suitable policy to overseas students. In Ontario only citizens and those with immigration status are covered, but Ontario universities have negotiated a mandatory private insurance plan for this purpose. The situation varies and is subject to change and you must always check the government's health care website which provides links to each province. You will find information on what is covered under the plan and whether you are covered when you travel. In some provinces, notably Saskatchewan the cost of medical care is covered entirely from provincial funds and in others, such as British Columbia, there is a monthly payment for the government healthcare scheme, but it isn't very much and students qualify for coverage after only three months. You must apply for cover and will find details and an application form on the above website or can obtain them from the university you plan to attend.

06 Getting a place

United States

■ What are my chances of getting a place?

If you can fulfil all the requirements discussed so far to at least the minimum standard, you have every chance of getting into an American university, as there are so many institutions in the United States that it is possible to find something suitable for everyone. You will need to be realistic about your chances of success, and match your academic and personal profile to those institutions to which you would like to apply. As is the case in the UK, some institutions are extremely selective and will require much higher grades. These will not, however, guarantee admission, as a great deal of attention is also given to personal statements, essays and references from teachers. Each institution has its own philosophy, and in some cases extra-curricular activities and outstanding references may outweigh high academic scores. If you feel that a particular institution is the right one for you, it is worth having a go – all you can lose is the application fee.

It may actually be more difficult to get into the most prestigious public universities than the most prestigious private ones. UCLA and UC Berkeley are examples of highly competitive public universities that attract a large number of well-qualified applicants who are California residents and must be given priority, as the University of California is a public institution receiving funding from the state of California. Athletic scholarships are an exception to this, as many large universities, both public and private, give high priority to inter-collegiate competition, and it is a coach's job to recruit the best, regardless of their country or state of residence. Private institutions have complete freedom so far as admission of international or out-of-state students are concerned, and will be looking for those students who most closely match their criteria.

The average acceptance rate at American colleges is 70 per cent, and 10 per cent of students attend colleges that were their third choice or lower. Harvard, Princeton and Columbia have the lowest acceptance rates at 9 or 10 per cent, with Stanford (11 per cent), MIT (13 per cent) and Brown (14 per cent) close behind. Liberal arts colleges with low acceptance rates are Amherst (Massachusetts) and Pomona (California), with 19 per cent and 18 per cent respectively. Colleges with a high percentage of international students include Wesleyan College (Georgia) at 17 per cent, Mount Holyoke (Massachusetts) at 16 per cent and Macalester, Minnesota and the University of Maine with 15 per cent each. This is the current position and subject to change. Remember that many highly competitive public institutions are limited in the number of students they can accept. Further information on acceptance rates can be found in the major guides and on websites.

If you are thinking in terms of applying for what is known in the United States as a *professional degree* – this includes Dentistry, Medicine, Pharmacy and Law – you should write at least a year in advance. It is extremely difficult for international students to gain places on these courses and you may be required to attend an American college for a year or more prior to admission. The number of places on such professional courses is severely limited and it is consequently also difficult for Americans. A good Bachelor's degree in an appropriate subject is required.

■ What are admissions staff looking for?

This will clearly vary, but here are the views of staff at one private and one public institution:

Harvard is highly selective and admits only one in ten applicants. As a private institution Harvard has no obligation to give preference to American citizens and aims to take the best students from all over the world. Academic qualifications and potential are, of course, very important, but Harvard looks for more than this. Students from the UK who are taking A levels are expected to get A grades in all subjects and have a full range of top-grade GCSE passes, but this is only the beginning. In the USA extra-curricular activities are considered to be very important and most of our students have reached a high level of achievement in at least one activity outside the classroom and can demonstrate leadership qualities. We look for students who will take full advantage of everything Harvard has to offer and give a lot back in return.

Lack of funds need not be an issue as Harvard is an exceptionally well-endowed institution and we are able to offer funding to any student who needs it. We have a formula for assessing the need, but do not look into a student's financial situation until we have offered a place. Our policy is to make offers to the students we consider to have the most potential and to be the most curious and open-minded and then we assess and meet their financial needs. We rely quite a bit on the references provided by the schools and on the essays the applicants write as they can tell us a lot about their potential. Students receive financial help according to their need and may also need to work or take a loan. Loans are available to international students but most prefer to work and can do this on campus for a limited number of hours. There are plenty of jobs on campus and students earn an average of $9.50 an hour.

We have an unusually high number of international students from around 80 different countries at Harvard and are fortunate in having specialist international admissions staff with knowledge of other education systems. The UK is one of the areas I deal with and I go there for up to ten days every year to visit schools and attend major higher education fairs. We have a volunteer outreach co-ordinator in the UK and work closely with the Harvard Club of the UK and with Pure Potential, an independent organisation set up to help bright students with their higher education applications. I receive requests to visit many schools and have covered quite a large area of the country. Harvard is actively trying to recruit bright students from state schools and has a network of alumni in the UK. Applicants have an informal interview with one of them as part of the selection process. Once we have gathered all the information, including the SAT results, an international admissions committee make an initial selection and then all 33 officers cast their votes. We don't require those whose first language is not English to take the TOEFL test as the verbal part of SAT 1 and the interview enable us to assess this. About one third of our applicants from the UK are entirely British, one third have dual American and British nationality and the remaining third have been educated in Britain but originate from other countries.

Harvard does not give sports scholarships as such, but does attract many outstanding sportspeople and we have recruited quite a few superb rowers from the UK. Those who shine in any area will stand out, but they must have the academic potential as well to be offered a place. Some of our coaches do travel to evaluate and recruit sports stars.

Students need to start thinking about applying in Year 12 and ensure that they register for the SAT tests in good time. The tests can be taken four times a year, but you must register six weeks in advance and take the tests by the January date prior to admission. It is possible for students to get credits for their A levels or the IB and it is possible to graduate in three years instead of four, but most students prefer to have the full experience.

In 2008 Harvard announced a 21.4% growth in its need-based scholarship aid, reducing the family contribution on a sliding scale for all on financial aid, down to zero for those earning less than $60,000 or equivalent.

Janet Irons, International Admissions
Harvard, Cambridge, Massachusetts

The University of California is a public institution with campuses across the state of California.

The University of California system does its own evaluation of foreign academic credentials. There is no charge for this and we ensure consistency is maintained by employing specialists on each campus who confer with each other in cases of doubt. Only around 5% of our students are from outside California, and we don't actively recruit for overseas students. Private universities have more freedom with admissions, as state policies must be adhered to by public universities. I recommend the website www.edupass.org for foreign students who want to study in the US as it contains a list of colleges indicating the number of foreign students at each, which makes it clear that these institutions welcome international students. At UCSB we currently have 62 British students: 7 undergraduates, 8 graduate and 47 exchange students. We can evaluate AS and A levels and don't need to see a syllabus. The IB is also well known to us.

We attach a lot of importance to the application form as we are looking for high achievers who are also well rounded, and look for evidence of extra-curricular activities such as athletics, music and community service. Most students apply using our electronic common UC application form on which students specify to which UC campus they wish to apply. Students may request a paper application if they wish. All students are required to submit an essay about themselves which is the equivalent of a personal statement. These are read by trained readers who use an established system of evaluation. We don't interview.

The University of California, like many universities, requires the SAT Reasoning Test and two SAT Subject Tests. I used to work at Mount Holyoke, one of the top all-female colleges, and they no longer use standard tests as part of the selection procedure as they prefer to put the emphasis on student achievement and believe that women can achieve more with a co-educational faculty that includes an equal number of female mentors.

Mary Jacob, Director of the Office of International
Students and Scholars
UCSB

Canada

There is no nationwide system of examinations in Canada and each university has its own entrance requirements. Most are familiar with the British examination system and with the IB and will assess you on an individual basis. In general the major universities will be looking for a broad range of GCSEs/Standard grades with A or B grades and A/AS or Scottish Highers/Advanced Highers at C or above. There may be a possibility of getting credits for high grades at some institutions and for some courses A or B grades are likely to be required. Most of the major universities specify the requirements in terms of UK and IB qualifications. McGill, in Montreal, for example, asks for BBC or better at advanced level and will give a maximum of 30 credits for top grades.

07 Getting your visa

United States

The Immigration and Nationality Act (INA) governs the admission of all people to the United States and the rules and regulations are always subject to change. Foreign nationals can be admitted to the United States as non-immigrants for a temporary period if they wish to pursue academic or vocational studies on a full-time basis.

Full-time and exchange students in schools (universities and colleges) approved by the US Citizen and Immigration Services are eligible to apply for F-1 or J-1 visas. The F-1 visa is for full-time students (minimum of 12 credit hours a week during each semester for undergraduates) at all levels, and the J-1 visa is for exchange students who are doing part of their course at an approved school in the United States. There is a charge for visas.

■ Essential documents

When you have been offered and have accepted a place at an approved university, you will be issued with a SEVIS (Student Exchange Visitor Information System) I-20 AB/ID form (if you require an F-1 visa) or DS-2019 (J-1 visa) by the school accepting you. This document is your proof that you are allowed to study at the institution indicated in the United States. The Department of Homeland Security charges a fee to support the SEVIS system. This is increasing to $200 by 1 October 2008 for non-immigrant students and is in addition to visa charges. Before you make an appointment to take the form to your nearest US consulate, you should check to ensure that the details are correct. If they are not, you will have to contact the university for a corrected I-20. The institution admitting you will also check bank statements or other sources of funding, and make a signed statement to this effect, to prove to the consulate that you have the financial resources required for the period in which you will be in the United States.

You also have to complete visa application forms DS-156 and DS-157, and males between the ages of 16 and 45 have an additional form to complete.

Accompanying family members must complete separate application forms and are issued with an F-2 or J-2 visa, which does not entitle them to work. The I-20 form gives your personal details (name, country and date of birth, country of citizenship), details of the school you are attending, the title and level of the course, the date of starting the course and the latest date by which it should be completed, the amount of money required and the source of these funds. These forms must be renewed and signed by the institution every time you leave the country. New legislation requires all visa applicants to provide a biometric identifier that can be encrypted on the visa. Fingerprints and photographs are then taken every time you re-enter the United States, and these are matched to the originals.

■ Consular interviews

Federal policy currently requires that all visa applicants have a personal interview with a consular officer. Applicants in certain categories may be required to undergo a security clearance, but this will not normally apply to British subjects. In practice, the interviews are usually very brief, but you may have quite a long wait at the embassy or consulate. You must make an appointment and cannot take large bags, mobile phones or other electronic devices into the Embassy. You must convince the consular officer that you intend to return to your home country after you have completed your course, and are advised to be prepared to answer questions about your reasons for wanting to do this particular course and why this degree is important to your career goals. You must ensure that all the documents required are in order, your passport is current and your photographs meet the required specifications (see Appendix 3).

■ Extensions to visas

Extensions are possible in certain circumstances, but these have to be applied for and approved. Requests for extension forms should be completed at least 30 days before the current permission expires. The international service at the university deals with all these issues and you must report to and register with them when you arrive. You must also keep them up-to-date with any changes in your circumstances.

You may have to wait some time for an appointment, and a further period (usually between 14 and 16 weeks) before you receive the visa, and should not, therefore, make any travel arrangements until you have done so.

■ Contact details

The US Embassy in London can be contacted as follows:

- Tel: 09042 450100 – these calls are charged at £1.30 per minute from BT landlines, but you are able to speak personally to an official.

Other networks and mobile telephones may charge more and the number may not be obtainable from some networks.

■ Post: The Consular Information Unit, United States Embassy, 24 Grosvenor Square, London W1A 1AE.

■ Website – www.usembassy.org.uk.

■ On arrival

When you arrive in the United States, you should receive Form I-94 (Arrival and Departure Record) with your admission number to the United States. This number will be written on your I-20 or DS-2019, and the immigration inspector will then send the first two pages of this form to your school as a record of your legal admission to the United States. You retain the remaining pages as your proof of entitlement and should keep these in a safe place.

F-1 visa holders may leave the United States and be readmitted after absences of five months or less. When you return to continue your full-time study you must have a valid passport and visa as well as a current USCIS I-20 ID.

You can avoid any major problems at immigration if you follow the rules and remember that immigration regulations are subject to change without notice. It is your responsibility to stay informed and take the required action, and there are international specialists at all institutions to advise you and help if you do run into any problems. You must keep the staff there informed of any changes in your programme or status so that they can maintain your SEVIS record. SEVIS is an inflexible system with zero tolerance for those who violate the terms of their student status.

Canada

▓ Getting your Canadian Study Permit

UK students going for more than six months to study require a Study Permit and must apply to the Canadian High Commission for this. The cost is $125 – about £70. This takes about six weeks to process. You need a valid passport, letter of acceptance from an educational institution and proof of sufficient funds to cover tuition, living expenses and medical insurance.

Students applying to a university in Quebec also require a Certificat d'aceptation du Quebec (QAC) which will cost an extra $100.

The Study Permit is issued by Citizenship and Immigration of Canada and application forms can be obtained from the website. You must have been accepted by a university or college before applying and should not make arrangements to travel until your application has been approved. You will need to provide:

- The completed application form (IMM 1294) and checklist.
- Your letter of acceptance from a Canadian institution.
- Evidence of funding in the form of original bank statements from a UK, Irish or Canadian bank and/or proof of a loan or scholarship. The minimum amount you will need to have available is the cost of tuition plus $10,000 for a 12-month period. Additional amounts are needed for accompanying family members.
- A copy of the identity page of your passport, which must be valid for the period your study visa is requested. British citizens do not need to send passports.
- Two passport-size photographs, signed, dated and taken in the past six months.
- The processing fee ($125). You cannot pay with cash, a credit card or personal cheque and must use a bank draft in Canadian dollars, payable to 'The Receiver General of Canada' and with your name and address on the back. A postal order in pounds sterling is acceptable if you are delivering your payment and forms in person.

You are not required to attend an interview and can do everything by post. If approved, you will receive a letter of introduction, which should be shown to the Canadian Immigration officials when you arrive. You will need to satisfy them that you will leave Canada when you have completed your course of study. You will then receive the Study Permit and are advised to note the expiry date and conditions. Do not let it expire. You must make sure that you renew it if you need to and should do so at least 30 days before it expires. If it expires and you have not applied for an extension you must leave Canada.

As long as both your passport and Study Permit are valid you may leave and return to Canada whenever you wish during your period of study and require no other documents.

If you decide to transfer to a course at another Canadian university you can normally do so without applying for a change to the conditions of your Study Permit, but it's always advisable to check this.

You can apply for a Study Permit even if you are only going for a few months, but it is not required for periods of less than six months. Some people choose to apply as it allows them to work on campus. If you are applying for this reason you need to submit a 'letter of explanation'.

If you are not a British or EU citizen you may also require a temporary resident visa and will need to apply for this, send your full passport and have a medical examination. There is an additional fee of $75 for a single entry, $150 for multiple entries and $400 for a family.

British students who will be going into hospitals, schools, daycare centres or similar service providers as part of their course will also need medical clearance.

More details can be found on the Citizen and Immigration Canada website and that of the Canadian High Commission in London.

08 Living as a student in North America

■ Finding accommodation

Many students and their parents worry quite a bit about finding accommodation and you are strongly advised to start making enquiries as soon as you are accepted at a university. There will be a housing officer who can provide information about the various options and costs. In many cases, information and an application form for housing will be sent to you with your acceptance letter. In some smaller colleges, accommodation may be available for all or the majority of students, but larger universities have more limited accommodation and you may have to find private housing. As is the case in the UK, every effort is made to offer campus accommodation to freshman students who apply early enough. It is usual for students to share rooms, and this is certainly the cheapest option.

■ Will I be allowed to work in the United States?

There are very specific federal regulations about this and you must be aware of them. International students are permitted to work for 20 hours per week on campus during the semester or quarter, and full time during breaks and the summer vacation. You'll need to get a Social Security Number (SSN) first and this could take some time. Off-campus employment is only allowed in the following circumstances and permission is required:

- Curricular Practical Training. Only work considered to be an integral part of your curriculum will be authorised. You must have completed a full academic year and obtain authorisation from your institution. Procedures for this will vary.
- Optional Practical Training. Only work that is directly related to your major field of study will be authorised. You will have to apply for an Employment Authorization Document (EAD) from the Bureau of Citizenship and Immigration Services. You will be issued with an Employment Authorization Card (for which you must supply an acceptable photograph – see Appendix 3) and it is only valid for 12 months.
- Economic Hardship. Off-campus work may be permitted in cases of sudden, unforeseen economic problems, if on-campus work is not

available. You must have completed one academic year on an F-1 visa before this can be considered.

It is important to be aware that there are usually very limited employment opportunities for undergraduates to work on campus and you should not rely on being able to obtain this to fund your studies. Most international students return home to work during the long summer break.

Working as a student in Canada

You are allowed to work on campus with a regular Study Permit and do not need a Work Permit. This includes working for a private contractor who is operating on the campus. After six months you can apply for an off-campus Work Permit, provided that your university is registered for this scheme and you are in good academic standing. All major universities and colleges in Canada participate in the scheme which allows international students to work off-campus. A full list of these institutions is on the website. Work permits cost $150 and allow you to work for a maximum of 20 hours a week whilst you are studying. You will also need a Social Insurance Number (SIN), similar to an SSN in the United States. As a non-resident worker your nine-digit number will begin with a '9' which indicates that it has an expiry date, usually the same as the expiry date for your Study or Work Permit. You can apply for a SIN at any Canadian Employment centre.

Spouses can apply for an open work permit as soon as you are in the country. There is a lot of information on both study permits and work permits on the Citizenship and Immigration Canada website (www.cic.gc.ca/english/index.asp).

Postgraduation Work Permit Program

In April 2008, the Canadian Minister of Citizenship and Immigration announced changes to work permits for international students to encourage them to study in Canada and then consider staying permanently if they meet the requirements. International students graduating from Canadian universities can now obtain open work permits for three years with no restrictions on the type of employment and no requirement to have a job offer. They must apply within 90 days of receiving written confirmation that they have satisfied the requirements of their academic programme from the institution they attended. This extension of postgraduation work permits will make it easier to apply to immigrate to Canada.

09 Undergraduate exchange programmes — an alternative option

■ An overview

As you can see, a full four-year undergraduate degree in North America is an expensive undertaking, except for the fortunate and talented few who are able to obtain a scholarship. You may be feeling that it is not for you, perhaps because of the cost, or because you don't want to commit to four years away from your home and friends, or you have concerns about the acceptability of an American or Canadian qualification. An excellent alternative option is to apply to a British university participating in a programme that offers the possibility of a year at an American or Canadian university. You can find information on exchange programmes in prospectuses and on university websites. In most cases they are available to students regardless of the subject they are studying, and grades received whilst in the United States may count towards the final degree. Where they do not count towards your final marks you will be required to pass. You will receive a transcript of your grades at the end of the year.

The terms and conditions vary according to the home and host university but, in general, students pay only half the home fees during their exchange year. As you would remain a student of the home university, the student loan is not affected and you are, in fact, likely to be able to take a larger loan. When you apply for your J-1 visa, however, you need to prove that you have around $18,000 available and cannot currently count the loan in this figure. A second-year student in the UK would take classes for third-year American students (known as upper division) and be regarded as a junior (third-year student), as this is the first year of study of the major subject. Your home university will expect you to select subjects appropriate to your degree, but you will also be free to take at least one other class of your choice. It's important to make sure that you register for classes quickly as students register online for them and they can fill up quickly. It's also important to find out about housing and sort this out in advance. Don't necessarily expect to be given this information – it's up to you to ask for it and do your own research on the university's website.

The following students are all on exchange programmes at the University of California in Santa Barbara (UCSB) studying under the University of California Education Abroad Programme (www.eap.ucop.edu) in which 12 universities in England and 4 in Scotland participate. All students commented on the excellent orientation programme which helped them to get to know and support each other.

■ Student experiences

This has been the best year of my life, despite the lack of pubs, which are the focus of social life at Sussex. UCSB is virtually on the beach and it's very easy to get used to the lifestyle and climate. I feel that I now understand Americans better and have made friends although I share a room with another Sussex student. We pay only half the home tuition fees and can increase our student loans. I've been lucky enough to find work promoting a website on campus and can work for 10 hours a week. My grades here will count as 20% of my final marks so I do have to take relevant courses, work hard and attend regularly. I find that it is easier to do well here, but you have to study consistently.

Emelia Goodfellow
American Studies, Sussex
(UCSB – www.ucsb.edu)

It's going to be really hard to leave here as the outdoor lifestyle means you feel healthier, take more exercise and feel very safe walking around at night. I found it strange that most students here share a room, but it does keep the cost down to $450 a month plus food. Students are friendly but you have to make the effort to get to know people. My grades here do not count towards my finals but I do have to pass and I am using some of the material as research for my dissertation. Nottingham has been very flexible about the courses I can take, although I have to keep them informed. I was, for example, allowed to take sociology and Spanish. Crashing courses has been a bit of a nightmare, but professors usually understand if you are an EAP student. There is a lower maturity rate and the lack of bars on campus and taking attendance make it more like school.

Emily Eaves
English and American Studies, Nottingham

I have to take 75% of upper division courses in History and these count as 40% of my final marks. The resources and sports facilities here are amazing and I have been a founder member of a new fraternity. This costs me $250 a quarter, but is great for social networking and I've made a lot of friends. I pay $875 a month for my room but this does include meals. I find the freshmen here are much more immature than in the UK.

Tom Clarke
History, Durham

I'm 26 and had to save a lot of money to enable me to come out here, but it's been well worth it. I knew I wanted to take full advantage of being here and didn't want to run out of money. As an independent mature student my LA provided extra money for me to study abroad and will also pay for up to three return flights and my medical and visa fees. My loan was also increased. The return flight money is available in case you need to get back for any special reason, but I recommend staying out here and taking advantage of the opportunity to travel. I was lucky to get into university accommodation at $475 a month as I couldn't have afforded private housing. It is a lot easier to get good grades here, but there is a lot of assigned reading followed by regular tests. I much prefer the system as it forces you to work consistently rather than put it off and then cram. Although the level is not as high I feel I am learning more. There is a wider choice of courses here, although you have to make an effort to get on some of them. EAP students with a GPA above 3 can petition to do a graduate course and I chose to do an independent study, which enabled me to raise the level of work required so that it was closer to the UK. UCSB is very flexible and actually created a course title for me. I found a tutor who was willing to do this independent study with me and have found it invaluable as it allows me a one-to-one meeting every week and has given me a much better understanding of how to approach a research topic, which will be really beneficial in my final year.

Cathryn Haigh
American Studies and History, Sussex

I chose (UCSB – www.ucsb.edu) because I wanted the California experience and the beach lifestyle defines that for me. I've found it so rewarding and made so many friends that I would push people to do a year abroad and will always want to come back here. My tutors were less keen for me to do it and it doesn't count towards my degree, but I have accepted that I will have to work flat out next year. It is more like school here with weekly homework and tests, but I like the fact that you get points for class participation and I've managed to do quite well and have a great social life.

Leonora Howard
Religious Studies, Edinburgh

I'm really glad I did the exchange year, but it hasn't been all positive for me as I'm not a big fan of the USA and find attitudes are very different. There is wide choice of courses here, but sometimes I feel that there is a lack of progression and I miss doing more in-depth essays. On the other hand there is a wide choice of courses here and I've really enjoyed travelling, the outdoor lifestyle and wildlife. The year counts as 50% of my degree and I do the other 50% when I return.

Lily Martin
Anthropology of Religion, Lancaster

This has been the best year of my life so far and I've found it very fast-paced although the level is lower and less challenging. The year doesn't count towards my final degree but I do have to take 50% of my courses in Economics and to pass. This means that I have been able to take courses in other disciplines and follow my academic interests. I wanted to study a foreign language and chose Arabic after using the website www.ratemyprofessors.com to find out about the teaching on the various UC campuses. I'm in university accommodation and pay $550 a month for a shared room. It's easy to make friends here although friendships can be more superficial and Americans refer to 'hanging out' with people rather than making definite plans. I have found that race and ethnicity are more prominent in how people define themselves and Americans tend to be more patriotic.

Nick Rose
Economics, Warwick

I would have preferred a university on the east coast, but got a scholarship to come here. As the year counts for 50% of my marks I have to take prescribed courses and this has sometimes been difficult due to course changes. As I'm from a university in Scotland I have no fees to pay, but had to work to have enough money to come here as US Immigration doesn't take your student loan into account when you apply for a visa. The courses are academically easier, but demanding. You are forced to work hard and this gears you up for your final year. There is a different work emphasis and it's easy to slip up, but if you keep on top of it there's no problem. The system is more like an extension of high school and there is more immature behaviour.

Graham Skalley
Psychology, St Andrews

TIPS

- Try to register as early as you can for courses as most people find they have to crash courses they need when they are full. Go to the class and talk to or email the professor and there is a good chance you will get on.
- Take advantage of the opportunity to travel – airlines can be expensive but Greyhound buses and Amtrak (rail) are cheap.
- Transport can be difficult and taxis are expensive, but there are often free bus services offering local transport for students.
- The visa process is quite complicated so make sure you apply early.

The student in the following case study is a participant in an exhange programme between the University of Cambridge and MIT in Cambridge, Massachusetts.

I am studying Economics at Cambridge University and in my second year, although I am a junior here. I've always wanted to study in the US and especially to have the experience of an Ivy League college. It looks good on your CV and MIT has the best Economics programme in the US. Being an exchange student is considerably less expensive as I continued to pay the £3,000 a year rather than the $50,000 cost at MIT. There are some additional costs of course as you need medical insurance, have flights to pay for and have to equip yourself with bed linen and other personal items since it is not viable to bring everything over. I got a £1,600 bursary to cover these costs.

Before applying for the programme I talked to previous students who had enjoyed the experience and I was chosen by Cambridge to participate in the programme on the basis of a personal statement, reference from the Director of Studies and my grades.

Getting the necessary J-1 visa wasn't a problem, but I did have to go to the US Embassy and wait in a queue for three hours for a one-minute interview.

Before going to Cambridge I attended Nonsuch High School for Girls in Surrey, a selective science specialist state school, where I obtained four A levels and two AS levels at grade A. I also achieved merits in the Advanced Extension examinations in Economics and Maths. At Cambridge I achieved a high 2.1 in

Part I of the Cambridge Economics Tripos and this all helped me to be selected for the exchange year and to gain a competitive scholarship position at MIT.

It has been an amazing experience, albeit MIT is incredibly intense. There are major differences between the Cambridge and MIT systems of learning and assessment and both have their advantages. At Cambridge you are under the supervision of experienced professors whilst at MIT you have 'recitations' by graduate students. The latter are more approachable, whereas professors at Cambridge seem to know everything. In addition to the core subjects in Economics, I have had the opportunity to take classes in taxation at Harvard Law School and classes in accounting at MIT's prestigious Sloan School of Management.

In the US you have to maintain a good grade point average as this is cumulative and determines your final result. You have midterm examinations as opposed to everything depending on third year finals as at Cambridge. This really boils down to permanent stress at MIT versus the killer final term at Cambridge. I have achieved a GPA of 4.7 and the whole experience has taught me a different way of life.

If you are thinking about participating in an exchange programme I advise you to find out as much as you can about the exchange university and make sure it suits your personality. You must also be willing to adapt your study techniques for a new type of education. You won't regret it.

Dharini Chellappah, Exchange student
MIT

I am studying History and Political Science as a joint honours degree at the University of Warwick and am currently spending a year on an exchange programme.

A big part of my decision to do an exchange year was the amazing experience I had from my Rotary Youth Exchange three years earlier. Also, I'm really active in sports, especially ice hockey and the university sports in the US are on a completely different level, both in quality and organisation. I enjoy meeting new people and I'm still in contact with most of my friends from my prior exchange.

In deciding where to do my exchange year I mainly used the information provided by the Study Abroad offices at both Universities and the UConn website was a fairly helpful resource. As I have relatives in the general East Coast area I was able to talk to people who had previously attended

UConn. I also contacted an exchange student from Warwick who was at UConn. I made the final choice based on the location and the fact that UConn was the only school of those I could choose from that had its own ice rink.

Although I did receive a bursary, there are a lot of expenses that most of the students coming from England wouldn't expect. The amount of money you need to purchase books for the courses is incredible and during my first semester I spent over $300 on books. I did have insurance that covered me in the US as well, but most of the universities require exchange students to take out their insurance. I think it was about $800 for the whole year. Travelling is always an extra expense, especially for breaks. Most of my friends went on trips about every two weeks.

Although I had no difficulty in obtaining my J-1 visa, there was a lot of paperwork to fill out. I had to wait for the form DS2019 to arrive from UConn and also had to pay the SEVIS fee and wait for the original document to arrive. I also needed proof that I have at least $12,000 at my disposal for the whole year and an assurance that my parents would 'sponsor' me. After I had assembled all the necessary documents I got an appointment at the US Embassy and went for the interview.

As an exchange student I was provided with accommodation on campus, but most of the university accommodation does not provide bed linen and other basics like a pillow, so you'll have to get those once you arrive.

One of the main differences I found is in the structure of the courses themselves. Most of the undergrad courses are not divided into lectures and seminars, but are a mixture of both and students are expected to participate in lectures. Most, if not all, of the courses only run for one semester so there are rounds of finals at the end of each semester. Teaching methods vary and it really depends on the individual tutor; there are professors that are no different from the English ones and there are some that are more like high school teachers. The level of study is slightly lower since people can change their majors and for some courses there is no requirement for prior experience so they are just too simple. The workload once again depends on the tutor but they usually expect more reading than in the UK. On the other hand, less preparation is necessary for the actual classes. There are usually midterm exams in October, some classes require students to write papers and those are similar to English essays but most of the professors give you a restricted list of books you can work with and don't permit outside research, but once again this depends on the module and the tutor.

It's been a wonderful opportunity for me to be able to take part in an exchange programme and I think it will help me to decide what to do after my bachelor's degree.

If you get the opportunity to do an exchange, you should do it. A lot of people I talked to are afraid of going into a completely foreign environment where you don't know anyone, but everyone I have met so far has been extremely friendly. On the other hand, it might not suit everyone as you have to be willing to make new friends and be outgoing.

Lukas Szabo, Exchange student
University of Connecticut (UConn)
(www.uconn.edu)

I had been on a trip to Canada shortly before starting my degree programme at the University of East Anglia. Although I hadn't specifically chosen my programme because there was an exchange option, when I saw that there was the chance to spend a year in Canada it seemed like a good opportunity. I was on a BSc course in Meteorology and Oceanography and the exchange offered was at a university in North America in the third year. I was in competition with other students at UEA for a place at the University of British Columbia in Vancouver, which was the most popular choice and probably the only place that really interested me. Places were allocated on the basis of personal preference and a submission justifying your choice. UBC was the only one available that offered a wide range of classes in my field of interest and it was also my first choice because I was keen to study in Canada rather than the US. I knew that Vancouver would be a fun place to spend a year.

I found out as much as I could to justify my choice and got my information from three sources: the UBC website, conversations with students at UEA who had already been on exchange, and a limited pack of information produced by my department at UEA. Probably the first two were the most helpful. I had visited Vancouver previously, but not UBC and didn't have an interview.

As far as the organisation is concerned, pretty much everything was down to me – travel, living expenses etc. I managed to claim something from my Local Authority (LA) for health insurance and travel, but it was only part of the total cost. I continued receiving my student loan whilst I was in Canada and had no additional tuition fees to pay as these were covered by the exchange agreement. Many of the costs were similar to those that I would have incurred in the UK, although I did have to pay for private health coverage for 3 months until I became eligible for the government healthcare scheme, which in BC requires the payment of a premium but is relatively inexpensive. All students get a UPass (transit pass), which helps keep costs down.

I needed a study permit but the procedure is very simple and is done through the Canadian High Commission in London for a fee of $125. You have to show you have enough money to support yourself for the year.

I chose to live off campus, although campus accommodation was available if I'd wanted. It took a bit of time and effort to sort out an apartment and everything that goes with it, but it wasn't a problem.

The biggest thing, as far as study is concerned, is that I felt very much on my own. At UEA I had an advisor who I was required to meet regularly whereas at UBC advice was available but only if you had a problem. The choice of classes was mine, whereas I had very little choice in the UK. The whole class registration process was a bit daunting at first, but much easier when I got to the second term. When I arrived at UBC I found it a little strange that students register for classes but can withdraw during the first month of term without it appearing on their record. I found that some of the popular classes filled quickly, but lots of people drop classes early in the term so it's worth asking if you can still join. There is also the option to "audit" a class (i.e. attend but not take the class for credit), which was new to me.

There are differences as far as classes and assessment are concerned and I experienced more-regular testing than in the UK, although it varied a lot. Some classes had weekly quizzes, others just a mid-term and final exam. Mid-terms were something that I never encountered in the UK, but almost every class I have taken in Canada has included one. Generally more of the mark is weighted towards work during the term with less on the final exam.

I found teaching to be almost entirely lecture-based, but this may be because of my science background. Class sizes varied a lot – from five up to about fifty, although I heard that some of the first year undergraduate classes can be in the hundreds. Overall I think that I have found the workload to be a bit more than UK undergraduate classes. Perhaps the biggest difference though is the variation in workload from one class to another. UK classes seem to be more standardised than anything I've encountered in Canada. The workload of my classes varied hugely, but generally I'd say that I had more homework than I had in the UK. Generally the work is more straightforward, requiring answers to questions rather than showing original thought.

Grades are generally higher than in the UK. At UEA a mark greater than 70% equated to a First whereas in Canada a mark of 90% is often required to achieve an A+. This doesn't mean that classes are harder, since the average marks are correspondingly higher. My grades at UBC were not really taken into account in the UK so it was just a matter of a pass or fail. I know that some other UK universities incorporate the marks into the UK degree but I was pleased that this wasn't the case at UEA as it meant that I didn't have to worry so much about marks at a time when I felt I was still adapting to the new life.

My advice to someone contemplating an exchange year would be to try to get a place at a university in a city that interests you, and where there are at least some classes directly related to your degree programme. I met people who were taking completely unrelated classes, and they felt that they were wasting their time. The year is about experiencing another country, but it'll feel even more worthwhile if you get some interesting classes as well. Be prepared for the registration, but don't panic if the class you want is full as there may be a chance if you email or go to see the professor.

UBC, like most universities, runs a great orientation programme for new international students. I found it a good way to meet other exchange students right at the beginning of the year and you should take advantage of this.

Make sure that you have sufficient money. There'll be nothing more frustrating than being in a fantastic place but unable to make the most of what it has to offer.

My year at UBC was one of the best years of my life, and I'm still in contact with people that I met. It cost me a fair amount, partly because I wanted to do things and see things whilst I was there, but it was worth it. Vancouver is regularly voted one of the best cities to live in the world, and it was fantastic to experience life there. Not many cities offer both beaches and ski-slopes within 15 minutes of downtown!

It took a while to adapt to a lot of things, but this wasn't a problem and all part of the experience.

Simon Higginson, Exchange student
UBC, Canada
(www.ubc.ca)

In fact Simon found the whole experience so valuable that, on completion of his undergraduate course, he decided to return to Canada for his PhD. You can read about his experiences as a postgraduate student several thousand miles away in Halifax on pages 105–108.

Part II
Graduate study

10 An overview of the opportunities

There are many more students from the UK on graduate programmes than on undergraduate programmes in the United States and Canada, mainly because the range of opportunities and the prospects of employment as teaching and research assistants make this an excellent and affordable alternative. In most cases, tuition fees are waived or reduced and there is a stipend for the work done, which is generally around 20 hours per week. This means that students take longer to complete a programme, particularly in the case of a PhD or equivalent doctoral programme. This is not surprising, however, as they are also required to take courses to broaden their knowledge. Most take these in the first two years and also work for a faculty member (usually their PhD adviser). The work is not guaranteed and you have to re-apply each year, but there are usually plenty of openings, especially in the sciences. You must remain in good academic standing.

Admission to graduate school is initially done at departmental level, and individual members of faculty have the discretion to use their funds as they see fit. Teaching Assistantships (TAs) are an important part of the training for doctoral students as many will go on to teach in higher education, and this provides invaluable experience. Tasks vary, but include some undergraduate classes, discussion groups and grading of student examinations and assignments. Students whose first language is not English will be required to pass a test of spoken English (in addition to any TOEFL requirements) before becoming teaching assistants. It is common to switch to a Research Assistantship (RA) in the later years as this involves helping with student research projects, which can be connected with their own PhD topic. Although there are more opportunities in the sciences, graduate assistantships are available in a range of other subjects, including languages, music, sports and political science. There are also some international fellowships and scholarships available (e.g. USUK Fulbright Scholarship Programme). See 'Fulbright Commission' in Appendix 2. MBA students, on the other hand, will usually find themselves in fierce competition for the top schools and will have to find their own funding.

Academic researchers, particularly scientists, are part of an international community, and many work collaboratively or have links with academics in other parts of the world. Graduate students frequently receive information about opportunities through contacts of their undergraduate university department, but many also use the internet or other sources of information to research their area of interest and track down any possible openings. Opportunities at postgraduate level are offered through the relevant department and not by the university admissions department, although they do act as an initial filter to ensure that students have what is required to get on the course. In the United States and for some courses in Canada graduate students are required to take the GRE or GMAT (for MBAs), which is the equivalent of the SAT for graduates, and will be expected to have a good Honours degree in the chosen subject. It may be possible for students with a BTEC HND to register for an MA if they get a good score in the GMAT or GRE. It is equally possible, however, that they would be required to take the final (senior) year of an undergraduate degree.

Graduate student experiences

I have just defended my thesis and received my doctorate after 5.5 years here at FSU. The procedure is a bit different here as anyone can come along to hear you give a talk about your work and then a committee of five professors ask you questions about it. It all went smoothly and I am now Dr Redshaw.

When I appeared in the first edition of this book I was just finishing my second year and starting to concentrate fully on my research after all the course work and teaching I did at the beginning. When I look back I can see how useful both of these were to me. The advanced courses I had to take really broadened my knowledge of the subject and I probably wouldn't have had that chance in England. I hope to make my career in the academic world and my experience as a teaching assistant (TA) should give me an advantage over candidates who have not had that opportunity. I also helped FSU students with their REU (Research Experience for Undergraduates) projects and outstanding high school students selected for Florida's YSP (Young Scholars' Program). I feel that my experience in the US has made me a more well-rounded person.

As a graduate student I received between $18,000 and $20,000 per annum and had my tuition fees waived and could manage on that. I shopped around for medical insurance and managed to obtain a cheaper policy than the one available to me through the university, but you have to be careful about this as it has to be approved by the university and may give you more restricted cover. I am now starting a post-doctoral position with the same professor and my salary will go up to $40,000. I had my F-1 visa extended after five years and can use this visa for one year as I can count my new position as Optional Practical Training. Towards the end of this year I will start planning my next career move. I expect to learn about what opportunities are available through connections I have made with people in my field of research, and resources such as the APS (American Physical Society) website. I will no longer be entitled to a student visa, but other types of visa are available. I have never had a problem with my visa applications or with immigration.

When I first came to Tallahassee it was to take up an elective period at an American university, which was available to me as an undergraduate at the University of Surrey and I was then on a J-1 visa. I met my girlfriend here at that time and we are getting married next year. Needless to say, I have never regretted my decision to study in the US and would encourage others to look at the options available.

Matthew Redshaw, PhD in Atomic Physics
FSU

I did my first degree in Chemistry at Imperial College in London and applied to a number of universities in the UK and US for my graduate studies. I particularly wanted to live in a city and Penn fitted the bill very well as it's so close to the centre of Philadelphia, one of America's oldest major cities. I've been here for five years now and will soon be completing so I'm applying to international companies for jobs and also looking at suitable opportunities for post-doctoral fellowships. The University of Pennsylvania is an Ivy League school and its excellent reputation should be an asset.

When you apply for graduate study in the US you apply to the relevant school or department and it's important to do your research very thoroughly. The application process is quite expensive so it's best to keep this to a minimum. It's a bigger time-commitment here than in the UK as you have to take quite a lot of courses, write a lot of essays and take examinations. It will take longer partly because of this and partly because it's usual to work for at least a year as a teaching or research assistant to get a stipend and fee waiver. I arrived in October and worked as a teaching assistant for the first year, which gives you very good experience and is a great advantage if you want to teach in the future. I started my research the following May and receive a stipend of $24,000 a year plus health benefits which is amongst the most generous in American universities. I have to pay tax on this. It is usual to take the GRE, but I was not required to do this. I had no problems getting the required F-1 student visa and was able to apply to the US Embassy in London for this as soon as I received official notification that I would be fully funded by the university.

In my first year I lived in the graduate house but now live in private housing. Many students start in the graduate house and this is a good way of meeting people and making friends outside your department.

Joe Swift, PhD Student in Chemistry
University of Pennsylvania, Philadelphia

I received my undergraduate degree from the University of Southampton and looked at universities in the UK and abroad before making my choice of graduate study. I relied heavily on advice from university faculty and staff, who provided much insight and information about the pros and cons of specific graduate degree programmes. I used prospectuses to get detailed information about both academic and extra-curricular opportunities available within each university and university programme. Assessments and ratings from independent sources, including the Times Higher Education Supplement, were often useful.

My decision to study in the US was primarily based on the high standard of educational excellence offered by MIT and WHOI for the degree programme and research that I am pursuing. However, I thought it equally important to consider standards of living and investigated possible financial constraints and difficulties. Funding for graduate research is often difficult to secure and I submitted several research proposals to Fellowship Programs that offer financial support. I am fortunate that my graduate research programme is fully funded and I receive both tuition expenses ($45k per year) and a salary/stipend ($25k per year). My studies would otherwise be prohibitively expensive. Many sources of funding are not open to foreign nationals studying abroad, so it is important to research these prior to committing to any degree program. The US educational system at the undergraduate and graduate degree level can be significantly more demanding than the UK-based system. The average term of graduate study in sciences is five–six years in the US, as compared to three–four years in the UK (I am in my fifth and final year). Although the US-based system is significantly longer, I feel my chosen studies will better prepare me for a career in science and research. I have found a significantly greater opportunity to travel for fieldwork/research, attend conferences and network with members of the academic community within the US system than I believe would have been available in the UK. These opportunities also factored into my decision to study at MIT and WHOI (although such opportunities may be highly variable and specific to any chosen degree programme). Requirements and/ or opportunities to take classes and to teach may be important both for your degree programme and to you personally. I had a requirement to complete a rigorous schedule of classes in years one and two, in addition to pursuing laboratory and field research. I have no requirement to teach during graduate research, although I did elect to help teach a full-credit class as teaching experience can be highly advantageous.

I had previously completed a summer research program at WHOI and had visited MIT during that time so I was very comfortable with the experience and had no second thoughts about moving to the US. Living in Massachusetts, I do not notice any significant differences in overall culture and attitudes (both in and outside of education) as compared to the UK.

My best advice to students considering entering any graduate degree programme, with consideration of hindsight, is "be proactive". All the information gathering you perform ahead of time will make your life easier – know about the academic expectations (and opportunities) for your specific graduate programme, know about the financial costs and support you can expect to incur, think about the whole spectrum of life in and outside of study. If you make good progress you can be rewarded with a wonderful educational experience. For me, personally, it was important to consider whether a higher education degree was absolutely necessary – I really wanted to be sure I was prepared to spend over five very demanding years as a student, particularly in a foreign country.

Oh, and one last thing – to enter graduate study in the US you have to take the GRE (Graduate Record Examination). At the time, this might seem like a waste of precious time (I had to travel 70 miles to the nearest testing centre) and money (the standard test was about $170/£90). However, it turns out these are actually quite important.

Paul Craddock, PhD student in Chemical Oceanography Massachusetts Institute of Technology/Woods Hole Oceanographic Institution (MIT/WHOI) Joint Program

I graduated from the University of Sussex with a degree in Physics and was interested in doing graduate studies in Atomic Physics. My undergraduate adviser suggested the University of Connecticut, a public university with a good research reputation in this field. The main UConn campus is in a pleasant rural setting and might not suit the dedicated city dweller, but major cities like Boston are reasonably accessible. I have American cousins in the area and that was very helpful when I first moved here. During my undergraduate degree I took advantage of the Erasmus (a programme to enable undergraduates to study for a period in another EU country) scheme and spent time at the University of Freiburg so I was used to doing some study abroad.

I am now in my 8th year, which seems a long time compared with the UK, but is acceptable here if your adviser is sufficiently happy with your progress to continue the financial support and you are able to renew your student visa. I have joint advisers, one of whom is a professor at the nearby Wesleyan University, which is a well-recognised private school. During my first two to three years

I was required to attend courses and maintain a GPA of 3.00, which equates to an average B grade. It is not a completely free choice as certain courses are required by the department. In order to graduate you must take two courses (six credits) per semester. It is hard work but I found them very useful and well worth doing. I had to take regular exams and do written assignments and tests, some of which I found very tough. Before officially becoming a doctoral candidate I had to go through an oral examination.

In addition to the time commitment of all the courses I work as a TA in Physics, which involves teaching lab sessions, taking discussion groups or homework classes and grading student assignments. I am paid $20,000 per year for this and my tuition fees are waived. You can also get some additional money from the school and your adviser to attend conferences. There are some service fees I have to pay which amount to about $1,400 per year and I am still deferring my UK student loans. I now have to pay tax as an American resident, although I was initially classed as a non-resident. You need a car as public transport is poor.

My first F-1 student visa was issued for the normal five years and I had to re-apply for subsequent visas. My second was for two years and I had to wait in a long queue and have a proper interview for this. My third and current visa is for a further five years.

There are many advantages to doing a PhD in the US, but you have to make sure you understand and comply with all the regulations, particularly as far as your visa status is concerned. You need to be aware that it will take longer, although I have probably taken longer than most. I wish that I had known that I would only be paid during the two main semesters and would have to look elsewhere for support in the summer. I was lucky as I did manage to get some summer teaching and my adviser was able to make up the money from his research funds. You should check this in advance, especially if you take up your graduate course without an assigned adviser.

I do sometimes miss the campus culture I was used to at Sussex, the pub life and English beer. I now have a good circle of friends here and found some good places to enjoy a drink, although I am always asked for my ID in new places, as you have to be 21 to consume alcohol. The culture is different here, but you soon get used to the unfamiliar events such as Spring Break where undergraduate students go a bit wild and march around the streets.

As it is such a rural area much of the social life consists of parties in each other's homes, but it's a great atmosphere and the friends I've made here will be friends for life. The International Center runs a lot of activities and if you take advantage of these they will help you to integrate.

Students should be aware that it's difficult to get credit at first and you need to borrow money in order to build up a credit rating. I leased a car and kept up the payments regularly to help with this.

Andrew Carmichael, PhD student in Atomic Physics
University of Connecticut

I did a four-year Masters course in Physics at the University of Salford and am now writing up for my MSc after two years at Florida State University. I may return to a PhD at a later stage but am taking a break as I did not get through the qualifying examination set by the physics department.

My main reason for looking at opportunities in the US was that the kind of experiments I wanted to work on use a special facility available at Brookhaven National Laboratory on Long Island. As I am interested in experimental rather than theoretical physics and knew the area I wanted to work in I looked around to find a suitable match for me and applied to fifteen universities, each of which cost me between $30 and $50. I felt that it was very important to choose the right place and the right adviser so I used a variety of information resources and visited a number of places. There is a lot of information on applying to American graduate schools and I found the American Institute of Physics' website (www.gradschoolshopper.com) gave a lot of comparative data on departments and used it extensively. I also used a book called Getting What You Came For: The Smart Student's Guide to Earning a Master's or PhD *which I found gave really useful advice. I narrowed down my choices to a few places listed in the top ten institutions in my field and chose FSU after looking at all the data and considering the cost of living. I knew I could live more comfortably here because of the low cost of living. I was also interested in Berkeley in California but was not accepted there, although they sent me a very helpful letter. I didn't score that highly on the Physics GRE, which I found extremely difficult as there were around 100 multiple-choice questions to answer and you had only two minutes for each. The general part of the GRE was easy and I did do well in that.*

The visa just involved completing forms and a five-minute interview at the US Embassy in London.

I decided that I wanted to live off the campus and used the website www.craigslist.org which covers Florida and has plenty of rental housing listed. I am paid around $19,000 a year and my rent is $620 plus utilities. I also get a fee waiver and that would otherwise cost me $20,000 a year. It's much cheaper to live in the Alumni Village but very basic.

The big difference between graduate programmes here and in the UK is in the number of courses you have to take. I may appreciate that in the future, but have not been happy with the amount of work I have had to do so far. It is really the homework rather than the courses that has been so demanding and time-consuming. Although I had covered some of the work during my undergraduate course and found some courses easier I found the mathematics involved in the homework very difficult and would spend nine hours a day on it. The workload was sometimes so heavy that I was spending 90 hours a week on it when I was taking three courses. Part of the problem was that I was not used to American-style problems, which are more abstract than I was used to, but things are better now that I am taking only one course. I have to maintain an average GPA above 3. There really is no equivalent in the UK and there were times in my first year when I wished I had stayed there. I just felt sometimes that there were too many hurdles to jump through.

Things did get a lot better when I started on my research project. I went to Brookhaven twice and worked as a teaching assistant and both my research and teaching went well. Although I am not progressing to a PhD at this stage I do not regret the time I have spent here and will stay in Tallahassee as my fiancé is here.

Simon Edwards, PhD student in High Energy Experimental Physics FSU

I did my first degree in Meteorology and Oceanography at the University of East Anglia and am now in the second year of my PhD course. Dalhousie is the major university in Halifax, Nova Scotia which is on Canada's east coast and very accessible from the UK. I wasn't mad about Halifax when I arrived, but friends said to give it a year. Sure enough I now don't want to leave.

It wasn't a difficult decision for me to choose Canada for my PhD as I spent a year on exchange in Vancouver during my undergraduate course. I really liked the country and decided that undertaking my grad studies here was a good way of 'trying' it out. When looking at courses I mostly used the web and couple of people at UEA had some knowledge of Dalhousie, which was useful.

As a mature student with a family to support, the financial compensation here is probably less than in the UK, but in Halifax the cost of living is considerably lower and we figured we could get a much better standard of living here whilst I study. Of course, the programme was also interesting. I only applied to one university in the UK as I found nothing else on offer that grabbed my attention, and the universities were in cities where I didn't want or couldn't afford to live. I would have considered the University of Victoria in British Columbia, but the cost of family housing was much higher.

I didn't visit Halifax before coming here, although I think a visit is worthwhile once you have narrowed your choice down to a particular school, but I had visited Canada on a number of occasions previously. All of my discussions with my supervisor were conducted by email. Possibly a risky approach, but it has worked out ok!

The application system seems to vary considerably. For my department there was a short online application form, which was very simple to complete and required no documentation. Once the department had identified me as someone who was of interest to them I was asked to complete a formal paper application requiring references and a transcript from my undergraduate degree. There is an administrator within the department who deals with all graduate study applications. A GRE wasn't required, although I know that some other Canadian schools do require it.

Getting permission to study is very simple – much more so than the US, I believe. I needed a letter of acceptance from Dalhousie and proof of funds (my offer of a scholarship seemed to be sufficient). The fee is $125 and the form is straightforward and was processed in London in a matter of a few weeks. I didn't have to go for an interview. The Canadian High Commission in London issues a letter and the formal Study Permit is issued on arrival in Canada, which took 15 minutes at immigration in my case. UK citizens don't need a visa, just the study permit – I guess that there may be a bit more paperwork for some non-UK citizens.

As a graduate student it's worth enquiring of your supervisor and other people in the department about accommodation options. I found that people here were more than willing to share opinions on areas to live and sources of rental information. Most people I know seem to have found it best to arrange temporary accommodation for the first few weeks, rather than tying themselves to a lease for a year on an apartment that might not be in the best location.

I have a scholarship from the school, which covers my tuition and leaves approximately $800 per month for living expenses. All students in my department who are accepted are offered a scholarship. I was unable to find any supplementary sources of funding for which I was eligible, as most require that you are either a citizen or permanent resident (landed immigrant). There are, however, some government benefits that students are eligible for and it's worth mentioning that healthcare is free in many provinces, but the rules vary from one province to another.

Here in Nova Scotia there's a one-year waiting period, necessitating private health insurance for the first year. The university offers a suitable policy to overseas students for about $650. Supplementary insurance (prescription drugs, dental etc.) is included for all students as part of the fees.

As far as the PhD programme is concerned the main difference for me is the requirement to take classes which generally increases the time required to complete, but I feel that I've gained a lot from the classes, so I don't consider this a downside. The number of classes you have to take seems to vary a lot, even within Dalhousie. For my department we're required to take a minimum of six classes though most people take more and I've completed eight. Generally we're encouraged to get them completed as soon as possible, preferably during the first year or two. A class here is three hours of lectures per week for one term. Be prepared for classes. I found my entire first year to be occupied with classes, with no hint of any research.

I was given a place with a supervisor that isn't tied to a particular research project. This suits me, because it has given me time to develop my interests, but is probably different from most UK institutions where you will probably be offered a place researching a specific topic. The department is research focussed and most professors have relatively little teaching. As a result I have no teaching myself and my time is spent entirely on research.

I haven't really experienced any problems adapting. Everything is a bit different from the UK, but that isn't really a problem. However if you come expecting everything to be the same you'll be disappointed. I think that a lot of things here are slightly more familiar to Brits than would be the case in the US – even the language differences are less. Of course there are the usual hitches trying to get used to a new city and a new university. I guess that's the appeal of moving to a different country to study – there are lots of new things to figure out and get used to. I guess that students here generally seem a little more academically-keen than their British counterparts. The social side of things is still important, but perhaps a little less dominant compared to the UK.

I have absolutely no regrets about my choice. It would be nice to have more money, but that's being a graduate student and nothing to do with Canada.

I would advise anyone considering graduate study in Canada to find out as much as they can about the options first and to take advantage of the very good International Student Services teams who will provide a lot of information. Don't expect things to be *arranged for you, but there are always lots of people that you can ask for advice. Don't expect to be special because you are an international student – there are lots of us!*

Don't panic if things don't seem great at first. It takes time to adjust.

Simon Higginson, PhD student Physical Oceanography
Dalhousie University
(www.dal.ca)

I graduated from the University of Plymouth with a BSc in Marine Biology and then went to the US and worked as a research and development biologist at the University of Mississippi for 18 months. I knew that I wanted to continue with my studies so I returned to the UK for a month and visited a number of universities to look at the research they were doing in areas that were of interest to me. I met my current supervisor and liked the sound of her research. She suggested that I should apply for a Canadian Commonwealth Scholarship as she was moving to Canada. As I felt that the research topic was more important than the place, I followed her advice and was successful so I was fully funded for the first two years with all tuition paid and a stipend of $1,200 per month. In addition I received a book fund of $800 and my moving expenses. I didn't have to take the GRE as Canadian universities don't normally require this and getting a study permit was no problem. Health care is not the problem it would be in the US as you are eligible under the provincial health programme after three months and this is reasonable at $50 per month.

I'm working on the pollution effects on tropical marine ecosystems in Saipan, Northern Mariana Islands, which belong to the US and are south of Japan and west of the Philippines. I spent six months carrying out my research, which involved snorkelling in a lagoon and surveying the health of the coral reefs. Initially I intended to do a PhD but things didn't work out quite as we wanted with regard to the research. I decided to do an MSc instead and will soon be completing this. It has taken three years, but I also had to take three courses in my first two years and these involved about ten hours of work per week. Although I had a free choice of courses there were not many applicable to my field so a couple of 'directed studies' courses were created for me and this was really helpful for my research. I have not done any specific duties so far but will be teaching for three weeks this summer at a marine research station on Vancouver Island and will be paid $4,000 for this. My supervisor will top this up to $6,000 as required by the biology department.

The main difference between doing an MSc in the UK and Canada is the time it takes, though in the sciences the longer time enables you to do more research and hopefully get more publications. Initially I wasn't too keen on taking more classes but I now realise it's important to continue with learning.

Vancouver is an expensive place to live, but after initially living on campus I used Craigslist and found it to be the best source of affordable accommodation. It's a good idea to start with campus accommodation as it gives you time to look around. I have no regrets about my decision to take my MSc in Canada but I would advise students to save up as much money as they can before starting a course.

I am now applying for jobs as a Tropical Marine Biologist in Canada and the US and have just applied for positions in Hawaii and Florida. I plan to work for a couple of years and then decide if a PhD is what I really want to do. It seems like an important thing to do if you want to go into academia, but I'm not sure that it will help me to get the kind of job I want.

Lucy Harrison, MSc in Tropical Marine Ecology
Simon Fraser University, Vancouver
(www.sfu.ca)

I did my first degree at the University of Bristol and chose to do an MBA in the US because of the large number and high quality of the business schools. I'm also adventurous and wanted to live somewhere new. I wanted to be sure I'd made the right decision so I looked at websites and business articles, spoke to students at the universities I was considering and visited them.

When I visited MIT Sloan I really liked the people and the environment. The location was important to me too and Boston is a great city. It seemed to be a perfect cultural fit so I applied and was interviewed for a place on the MBA programme. I was accepted and MIT facilitated the visa application process, which was a big help. Applicants must formally apply for the visa in person at the US Embassy and have a brief interview. They require proof that you will have sufficient funds whilst you are in the USA and MIT Sloan makes it easy for MBA students to borrow the full cost of tuition and living expenses from CitiBank. All my tuition and living expenses are paid for by graduate loans. I am aware that I will have a debt of $150,000 ($85,000 tuition and $65,000 living expenses) when I graduate, but I anticipate paying this off in five to ten years.

It wasn't difficult for me to find somewhere to live as most US universities have plenty of dorms/halls of residences so it's easy for first years to find accommodation on campus.

109

I have to take between five and eight courses per semester in order to get the credits required to graduate and there is a heavy workload with lots of assignments and exams. One of the advantages of the US system is that there is a large choice of classes. The universities I have seen here are very well funded so facilities are way better than those at most UK universities.

The main disadvantage of the US system, at least for those on an MBA programme, is that it is expensive and not easy to find any source of funding other than loans. The US culture is completely different and the teaching culture and methods are also very different, but I managed to adapt well to both.

I advise anyone considering studying in the US to visit the universities before selecting where to apply as the environments, cultures, campuses, towns and also the people can be very different.

I have absolutely no regrets about my choice. Studying at MIT has been the experience of my life.

Simon Harwood, MBA student
MIT Sloan School of Management

I graduated with a BEd from Bangor University and applied for a teaching post at a British international school in Kiev after spotting an advertisement in the Times Educational Supplement. I'd specialised in primary education and liked the concept of international education so I spent a year in Kiev teaching 6 and 7 year olds which I enjoyed. I quickly became aware, however, that a first degree isn't enough if you want to advance in international education and began to think about a higher-level qualification. It was really by chance that I applied to Florida State University as I knew someone here and decided to look at their website. I was quite excited to find this two-year course in the Department of Education Leadership and Policy Studies and visited Tallahassee once to have a look at the city before applying.

I then began the rather daunting application process, which was complicated by the fact that I was living in Kiev where communication is not so easy and I spent quite a bit of money sending papers by FedEx. I discovered that I had to take the GRE and that was a bit of a nightmare as I was not familiar with some of the assessment methods. I failed it first time and paid to take the practice tests which you can do from a CD or online. This was definitely worth it and I strongly recommend that applicants take the GRE seriously and prepare for it. It was a hurdle but I succeeded and was offered a place. There is quite a lot of paperwork and initial expense involved and I had *to pay an agency to present my qualifications in GPA format so that I could provide FSU with a transcript of my qualifications. There are several recognised companies offering this service and I selected one from the US Government website*.*

My course has only a few students so my classes, consisting mainly of seminars and discussion, are quite small and usually take place in the late afternoon or evening as many students are working. We have quite a few essays to do and also presentations on our work – 20% of the marks are for class participation. My adviser gave me quite a wide-ranging list of course to choose from and I am taking three per semester, which equates to 9 credit hours – another system I had to get to grips with. This semester I am taking Education and Culture, Multi-Cultural Education and International Development in Education and will have to select different subjects for the next semester. There are, of course, required subjects such as statistics, which I avoided this semester. It took me a while to get used to the grading system. I was quite happy to get a B+ for my first assessment but soon found out that you are expected to get A grades, which is achievable if you work. The professors make it very clear what is expected of you and if you follow the guidelines and do the work you will succeed. It is perfectly possible for everyone to achieve an A grade which is not the norm in the UK.

I was very lucky to be offered a job helping in the International Center at FSU as this pays me $5,000 a year (paid twice-monthly during semesters) and qualifies me for tuition fee waiver. As a foreign student I am only allowed to work on campus and for 20 hours a week. I still have to use some of my savings as I run a car and chose to live in a two-bedroom apartment off the campus which costs $660 a month, but it is probably less expensive for me to study here as I have the fee waiver and a job.

My main advice to graduates thinking in terms of postgraduate study in the US is not to be put off by any of the procedures you have to go through prior to admission as it is very accessible once you get down to it. There is a lot of paperwork and the GRE and visa application processes are stressful, but it is well worth perse-vering. Before my interview at the US embassy I had to collect a lot of information together and prove that I would be financially independent. I found the visa application confusing at first, but everything worked out fine in the end and. I certainly have no regrets about coming here and urge other students to think about broadening their experience. It is a different culture here, but if you approach it with an open mind and take advantage of the opportunities offered you will find it very rewarding.

**Note:* Please see page 48 for details of companies offering this service.

Although I fell on my feet without doing a lot of research into courses, I would advise students to look at the very wide range of courses available in the US and to be aware of marketing techniques as glossy brochures can be misleading.

I may eventually decide to go on to a PhD, but I would like more international employment experience first as I haven't yet clearly defined my research interests.

**Karl Prudhoe, MA student in
Social, Cultural, International Development in Education
Studies (SIDES) – at Florida State University (FSU)**

The following mature student is on a 'cost-recovery' course, which aims to make some money for a university. He receives no funding, as is common for this type of course in all countries.

I am a mature student in Canada and did my first degree in Business Administration at Brunel University some years ago. After this I worked for ten years in the scuba diving industry in various positions, working my way up to be an Instructor Trainer, and then Director of Professional Training for a resort in Central America. At this point I felt that I needed a Masters to further my education in this field and to improve employment prospects outside the diving industry.

When I decided to return to study I knew that I did not want to continue to study or live in the UK and used the Internet to find out about courses available in Canada. I also asked my previous university for recommendations and looked at the quality of programmes before making my decision. I discovered that living costs in Canada are lower than in the UK and this was another factor in my decision. As I already had a degree and management experience it was not difficult to obtain a place on the course and an interview was not required. The application process for the required study visa was quite straightforward.

As I am doing an MA rather than a PhD it is not easy to find funding to cover your tuition and living costs and I am paying everything myself. I am now in the second year of a two-year course. I completed 8 courses over two terms, followed by one term of 4 courses, and I am now half way through another term of 4 courses. I then have an internship, and then the option of either a project paper or a 3rd term of 2 courses and a research paper.

I have found that you have more independence and less guidance in Canada, which may suit some students but has been more of a disadvantage for me. Unfortunately the course is not what I expected, and seems to be more of a money-maker for the faculty due to the current trend and interest in e-commerce. I think that North American universities are more dollar-orientated and business-minded than UK universities and I recommend talking to current students before committing. That is my regret. I must stress, however, that the individual classes have been good from the Management School and my criticisms are more directed at the Faculty of Computer Science who seem to neglect this programme; an impression shared by other people on my course. I am grateful that I can get credit with this Masters to do an MBA at a later date if I so choose.

I like Canada. It has a really nice lifestyle with a wide range of recreational activities.

Andy Phillips
MA student in Electronic Commerce

■ Differences in the US, Canadian and UK systems

The post-graduate students highlighted the following differences in the US, Canadian and UK systems:

- It takes quite a bit longer to achieve a PhD in the United States and Canada. In the UK, postgraduates doing research are not generally required to take set courses, but they do specialise at an earlier stage and spend three years on their major subject, making it more likely that they will start graduate programmes with a more in-depth knowledge of their subject. In North America all postgraduate students are required to take a specified number of courses, which are usually selected in consultation with their supervisor/adviser. In order to maintain funding, a specified GPA (at least B grades) will normally have to be maintained.
- There is a difference in grading philosophy, and it is more common to get A and B grades in the United States than it is to get a first or upper second in the UK. The academic work, although demanding, tends to be easier, and it is not difficult to get straight A grades if you study.
- Almost all postgraduate students in the United States and Canada work up to 20 hours a week as teaching or research assistants, which is another reason it takes longer. As well as helping to finance your course, it gives you invaluable experience – PhDs from the United States and Canada are highly regarded because of the teaching experience.
- You have to take the GRE (or GMAT for the MBA) at a recognised test centre. Testing is online and includes Maths, critical reading and writing skills, logic/problem solving and comprehension. Different universities and courses require different scores, and results are sent automatically to any university you have applied to. This will

not necessarily be required by British students attending Canadian universities.

TIPS

- It's important to start preparing early – at least a year in advance – as there are so many options and universities. There is a great deal of information on websites, and it is worth using them extensively to track down courses. Don't be put off by the length of the process.
- It's also important to research your future adviser as much as you can and make sure you agree on funding, research allowances, conference funding and other needs before you start. One student had a lot of problems and didn't feel that the supervisor provided all the funding and support required.
- The opportunities for funding postgraduate study are not widely known, so make the effort to seek out the information. There are many teaching and research assistantships, especially for scientists, and these are not publicised enough. Many students are simply not aware of them.
- As the grading system is very different in the United States, it can be helpful to send an explanatory letter with your graduate school application. The grading system is also very different in Canada but most universities there are familiar with the British system.
- Don't be put off by the length of the course as you learn a very wide range of skills.
- Don't be put off by having to take the GRE. It's very different from the exams usually taken in the UK and practice tests are recommended. There are many books to help you to prepare for the tests. You can also buy a CD to test yourself before taking the official GRE, or do practice tests online.
- If you are a postgraduate on tuition waiver, make sure that you keep up with this as it's renewable annually.
- To keep your F-1 status you have to remain a full-time student, so you can't take a semester off as an American student might decide to do.
- You won't feel at home immediately, but Americans and Canadians are very friendly and you soon will if you give it a chance.
- Make sure you stick to the rules and stay on the right side of the law to maintain your visa status.
- Remember to ensure that you have all the supporting paperwork whenever you leave the country or you will have a problem getting back in.

- Make sure you keep up with all your courses and maintain a good GPA.
- If you are on a PhD programme, try to complete all your courses in the first two years so that you can concentrate on your research project in your final years.
- Make good use of the US Educational Advisory Service (Fulbright). They have a vast range of information. You can also send them a draft of your personal statement and it is worth paying for their very helpful advice.
- It is worth looking at the Princeton Review website (www. princetonreview.com) and www.collegeconfidential.com as there are discussion sections for students and you can post questions.

Appendix 1 Common terms and abbreviations

Although you will be familiar with much of the terminology and commonly used abbreviations in the British education system, you may find those used in American college guides and in correspondence bewildering at first. The following list may help you to get familiar with some abbreviations and terms.

■ Abbreviations

ACT	American College Test – an alternative to the SAT
AP	Advanced Placement – a test for able students in some American high schools
BCIS	Bureau of Citizenship and Immigration Service (part of DHS)
CEEB	College Entrance Examination Board
CFR	Certification of Financial Responsibility
CLAST	College Level Academic Skills Test
CLEP	College Level Examination Program
CPT	Curricular Practical Training (employment required as part of a degree course)
DHS	Department of Homeland Security (US Immigration)
EAD	Employment Authorization Document
EAS	US Educational Advisory Service (based at Fulbright Commission in London)
F-1 Visa	The type of visa required by full-time international students in the United States
GED	General Educational Development – an alternative test equivalent to high-school graduation diploma for mature students
GMAT	Graduate Management Admissions Test
GPA	Grade Point Average
GRE	Graduate Record Examination – test for graduate admission in the United States
I-20 form	Your proof of acceptance to study at a US university or college

IELTS	International English Language Testing System
INA	Immigration and Nationality Act
J-1 Visa	The type of visa required by exchange students in the United States
LSAT	Law School Admissions Test
MCAT	Medical College Admissions Test
OPT	Optional Practical Training
SAT	A standard test to determine potential for undergraduate study in the United States
SEVIS	Student Exchange Visitor Information System – a national database to record and track overseas students
TOEFL	Test Of English as a Foreign Language – also commonly used in the UK
USCIS	United States Citizenship and Immigration Services

■ Terms

Credit Hour	The number of hours of teaching per week for each credit (subject)
Early Action	A scheme under which some US universities agree to give an early decision to high-achieving students who apply for this
Early Decision	A scheme under which students make a firm commitment to accept a place at a US university if offered
Electives	Subjects which are not mandatory but award credits towards a degree
Federal	The national government
Freshman	First-year student
Greek Life	(or Greek organizations) – student fraternities (male) and sororities (female)
Internship	A period of practical training which carries course credits (see CPT)
Junior	Third-year university student (first year of major subject study)
Liberal Arts	A broad range of subjects in which passes are required to graduate
Major	Specialist subject studied intensively for the final two years
Minor	Secondary specialist subject
Public school	School run by the state (others are known as private schools)

Resumé	Curriculum Vitae (CV)
Review	To revise for examinations or tests
School	Any full-time education institution, including universities and colleges
Semester	College or university half-year (system now used by some universities in the UK)
Senior	Final year of undergraduate studies (term also applied in high schools)
Sophomore	Second-year student
State	This refers to an individual state of the United States of America

Appendix 2   Sources of information

A good starting point is the US Educational Advisory Service, a government-funded service based at The Fulbright Commission, Fulbright House, 62 Doughty Street, London WC1N 2JZ. The opening hours are from 1:30 pm to 7:00 pm on Mondays and 1:30 pm to 5:00 pm on Wednesdays and Fridays. It is not necessary to make an appointment to use the comprehensive library. It is not a placement service, but holds regular free information seminars on topics such as undergraduate study (includes SAT and ACT information), graduate study and sport scholarships, and organises pre-departure orientation sessions. Dates and registration on the website. Book early.

Other services include a 30-minute advisory interview (£10), an essay-review service (£30) and a comprehensive application-review service (£75).

Email: education@fulbright.co.uk
Tel: 020 7404 6994
Website: www.fulbright.co.uk

There are also Regional Information Centres in Manchester, Glasgow, Edinburgh, Swansea and Belfast, offering a walk-in service only. Five of the six are based in university careers centres and all hold directories for the current year. They have websites, but do not offer telephone or postal advice or information. The addresses and hours of opening can be found on the website given above.

- Secondary Information Centres which hold the previous year's editions of directories are based at the Universities of Birmingham, Dundee, Hull, Plymouth, St Andrews and Ulster (Londonderry).

Other useful websites

It is important to recognise that many of the websites you will find are either not very reliable or are more concerned with promoting particular institutions or services in the private sector. It is not worth spending your time and effort on these if you are looking for a comprehensive listing of the opportunities available. It is best to stick to official websites. Some of the others do contain useful information but should be used with caution and selectively.

■ http://educationusa.state.gov – US Department of State website which covers types and choices of institution and provides a useful checklist and pre-departure information.

■ Comparative information on American institutions

■ www.petersons.com/educationusa – keyword or name of institution search to locate information on colleges/courses and for details of publications listed below. Also includes a range of additional information such as historically black colleges. The site is funded by the US government and is a reliable source of information. Further information (SAT, ACT and financial aid) can be found on www.petersons.com by clicking on 'International Students'.

■ www.univsource.com – select university by name, by state or by programme. Lists single-sex colleges and historically black colleges. Not an official site and lists private sponsors first – use with care. Includes Canada.

■ www.a2zcolleges.com – facility to search for specialist colleges, non-specialist institutions offering majors subjects such as Drama, Music and Art, and colleges with religious affiliations. Also covers Canada and the UK and includes elementary and high schools.

■ www.globalcomputing.com/university.htm – can select university by first letter of name or by clicking on the required state on a map.

■ www.collegeboard.com – provides a range of information including College MatchMaker. A facility to compare up to three colleges can be found at collegesearch.collegeboard.com/ search/sidebyside.jsp.

■ www.collegeprowler.com – the alternative college finder (subscription service).

■ www.collegeconfidential.com – range of information on colleges and facility to post questions on the site.

■ www.usnews.com (then click on 'Rankings & Guides') – gives information on accessing rankings with regard to the number of international students, the top schools, the lowest acceptance rate, the highest graduation rate and the highest proportion of classes under 20. The site gives only the top three and then provides information on purchasing the more detailed publication.

■ www.allaboutcollege.com – a site for American students which links to higher institutions worldwide. Also contains a 'college chat' facility.

- www.auap.com – produces annual rankings of US universities for international students (you have to register to access this part of the site) – offers a priced course selection service and a selection and guaranteed admission service.
- www.commonapp.org – for information on the common application form used by some institutions.

Test information (SAT, ACT, GRE, etc.)

- www.princetonreview.com – section on choosing a school and preparing for the SATs with free practice test and online demo. Has an international student section. See page 125 for publications.
- www.barronseduc.com – Barron's Educational, a publisher of many college guides and test preparation guides. See publications listed in the following page.
- www.kaplan.com – contains information on undergraduate, graduate and professional programmes and test-preparation materials.
- www.collegeboard.com – information on SAT tests and on financial aid for international students.
- www.act.org – information on ACT tests.
- www.fairtest.org – information on colleges which may exempt from standard tests.
- www.gre.org – information on GRE tests, practice tests and registration.
- www.mba.com – information on the GMAT tests.

US life and financing your studies

- www.iie.org – click on 'Opendoors' to access lists of institutions with the most international students – site of the Institute of International Education. Links to sister site www.fundingusstudy.org.
- www.edupass.org – section for international students applying to US colleges. Gives sound advice on choosing a school and lists those with most international students (top 50), highlighting those offering financial aid to international students.
- www.petersons.com – has an International Scholarship Search.
- www.prospects.ac.uk – information on study abroad for graduates
- www.InternationalStudentLoan.com.
- www.InternationalScholarships.com – searches exclusively for scholarships for international students.
- www.scholarships.com – matches students to scholarships.
- www.fastweb.com – free scholarship and college search.
- www.collegeboard.com – search for scholarships. Click on 'Pay for College'.

- www.ncaa.org – the official website for athletic scholarships.
- www.finaid.org/otheraid/sports.phtml – financial aid for student athletes website.
- www.uscampus.com – covers all aspects of studying and living in the USA – includes advice on applications and getting accepted.
- www.lifeintheusa.com – a guide to American life.

Immigration information

- http://uscis.gov – immigration services of the Department of Homeland Security.
- www.ice.gov/sevis/ – provides information on SEVIS (Student and Exchange Visitor Information System).
- www.unitedstatesvisas.gov – a new website which is the official source of information about US visa policy and procedures.
- www.usembassy.org.uk – provides an overview of the types of visa required. Click on 'Visas to the US', then 'Nonimmigrant Visas' and scroll left of screen – F-1 visas (full-time students) are covered under 'Students' and J-1 visas (exchange students) under 'Academics & Researchers'.
- www.TSATravelTips.us – the official Transportation Security Administration's site for packing tips.

Individual university websites

If you know the name or location of institutions you are interested in, you can either use a major search engine such as Google or try the common format of www. followed by the name of the institution (in full or abbreviated) and then .edu.

Some useful publications

Major directories

These provide useful information and statistics on over 2,500 colleges to enable students to compare institutions and assess their chances of acceptance. There is an increasing number of these directories, but the main publishers are Barron's Educational, Peterson's (a division of Thomson Learning), the Princeton Review, Fisske, US News and ARCO (also Thomson). Website addresses are given in the previous section.

- *Barron's Profile of American Colleges*, Barron's Educational
- *Peterson's Four-Year Colleges* – includes Canada

- *Peterson's Two-Year Colleges*
- *The Complete Book of Colleges*, Princeton Review
- *College Handbook*, The College Board
- *US News Ultimate College Guide*

Selective directories

The above publishers also produce selective directories covering the top colleges, colleges for students with disabilities or other specific areas. See websites.

Alternative directories

These give student views and information on social and other aspects of college not generally covered in other guides.

- *Students' Guide to Colleges (Top 100)*, Penguin Books
- *The Insider's Guide to the Colleges*, Yale Daily News (www. yaledailynews.com/books)
- *Untangling the Ivy League*, College Prowler
- *The Big Book of Colleges,* College Prowler
- *Uni in the USA*, Lucas Publications – UK student view

SAT and ACT tests

Guides to the tests and how to prepare for them

- *The Official SAT Study Guide for the New SAT*, The College Board
- *The Official Guide for all SAT Subject Tests with CD*, The College Board

Many other publishers provide guides, including Peterson's, Barron's, Kaplan and the Princeton Review. Details from websites.

Scholarships and other sources of finance

Consult websites – there are various Peterson's and other guides.

Help with TOEFL tests

For students who have not been educated in the English language

- *The Official Guide to TOEFL*, Educational Testing Service

Publishers such as Barron's, Peterson's and Princeton Review also publish guides.

Note: Many of the above are available at the Fulbright Commission in London, although they are not always the latest editions – see above for contact details and opening hours. To order other publications consult publishers' websites for information. Whilst guides providing details of rankings, average grading of students accepted, etc. are useful, the statistics given should be treated with a certain amount of scepticism. Do not rely on rankings of institution by quality, as there are no such official rankings, and the methodology used to assemble this data is inconsistent and subjective.

■ Sources of information – Canada

Official guide

Directory of Canadian Universities (DCU) – published by AUCC (www.aucc.ca/dcu)

Useful websites

- www.aucc.ca – Association of Universities and Colleges of Canada (AUCC) – provides general information on studying in Canada, which includes information for international students. Also administers some scholarships. This is the official website for the 92 member institutions – all major higher education institutions in Canada are listed and links provided to their websites.
- www.accc.ca – Association of Canadian Community Colleges (ACCC) – all listed institutions are public, but they are usually smaller in size than the AUCC members and typically focus on vocational diploma and certificate courses, although some of them do now offer degree programmes and students can transfer to degree courses. 'Community College' is a generic term and many have other names such as 'institute of technology' or 'university college'.
- www.cbie.ca – Canadian Bureau for International Education (CBIE) – provides information on scholarships and studying abroad.
- www.cois.org – Canadian Higher Education Committee (CHEC) – this is part of the Council of International Schools (CIS) and produces resources on studying at Canadian universities and organises educational tours.
- www.cic.gc.ca/english/index.asp – Citizenship and Immigration Canada – provides lots of information on study permits and work permits.
- www.canada.org.uk – the website of the Canadian High Commission in London – provides information on immigration, work and study requirements.
- www.cicic.ca – Canadian Information Centre for International Credentials – provides information on admission to universities and

colleges in Canada and contains useful fact sheets for students educated in other countries.

- www.studyincanada.com – produced by EDge Interactive, a Toronto-based provider of information services and software for the education community. It contains links to many colleges and you can find specialist institutions which are not members of AUCC or ACCC. The order in which they are listed bears no relation to their quality and it should be used with some caution. It is a useful website but membership driven.
- www.studycanada.ca – provided by the CEC (Canadian Education Centre) Network. The UK does not have a CEC. Includes scholarship information.
- www.universitysport.ca – information on scholarships and sport.
- www.edu-canada.gc.ca – a government website which provides details of courses, education costs and study permit and visa requirements for international students.
- www.immigration-quebec.gouv.qc.ca – information for those planning to live, work or study in the province of Quebec. In French, but English version can be requested.
- www.considercanada.com – a government website which provides useful information such as fees for international students in the various provinces. Links to the AUCC database of universities.
- www.arucc.ryerson.ca – Association of Registrars of the Universities and Colleges of Canada (ARUCC).
- www.isep.org – describes the system of education in Canada under 'Country Handbooks', but is more of a comparison between the United States and Canada.
- www.canlearn.ca – a Canadian government website which provides details of awards given to Canadian and international students.
- www.ouac.on.ca – Ontario Universities Application Centre – the central application service for undergraduate courses in Ontario.
- www.bccampus.ca – the post-secondary application service of British Columbia – the University of British Columbia (UBC), arguably the major university in the province directs applicants to www.you.ubc.ca – check individual websites for guidance.
- http://www.hc-sc.gc.ca/hcs-sss/medi-assur/res/links-liens_e.html – links to health services by province.
- www.cra-arc.gc.ca – Canadian Revenue Agency Home Page.
- www.universityaffairs.ca – a well-respected source of higher education news and information in Canada. Mainly for faculty and graduate students.

Appendix 3   US immigration photograph specifications

Photo Format for Visa Applications

**In order to avoid delays in visa processing,
please be sure your photo adheres to these standards**

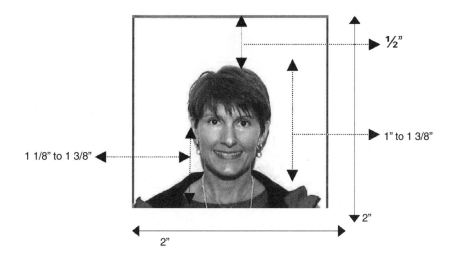

The photograph should be:

- taken within the last six months;
- 2 inches (50 mm) square, with the head centered in the frame. The head (measured from the top of the hair to the bottom of the chin) should measure between 1 & 1 $\frac{3}{8}$ inches (25 mm to 35 mm) with the eye level between 1 & $\frac{1}{8}$ inch to 1 & 1 $\frac{3}{8}$ inches (28 mm and 35 mm) from the bottom of the photograph;
- In color, or black and white against a white or off white background. Photographs taken in front of busy, patterned or dark backgrounds are not acceptable;
- unmounted, full face, with the face covering about 50 per cent of the area of the photograph, In greneral, the head of the applicant,

including both face and hair, should be shown from the crown of the head to the chin on top and bottom, and from hair-line side-to side. It is preferable that the ears be exposed;

- Head-coverings are acceptable only when the applicant's face is completely exposed;

- May contain a small (one quarter inch) white border on one side.